# BIOSCOPE

Diptakirti Chaudhuri is a salesman by day and a writer by night. His primary passion and subject of writing is Hindi cinema, on which this is his fourth book.

He lives in Bengaluru with his wife, son and daughter. They don't share his obsessive love for Hindi films. Yet.

# BIOSCOPE

## A FRIVOLOUS HISTORY OF BOLLYWOOD IN TEN CHAPTERS

DIPTAKIRTI CHAUDHURI

hachette
INDIA

First published in 2018 by Hachette India
(Registered name: Hachette Book Publishing India Pvt. Ltd)
An Hachette UK company
www.hachetteindia.com

1



ISBN 978-93-5195-228-2

Hachette Book Publishing India Pvt. Ltd
4th/5th Floors, Corporate Centre,
Plot No. 94, Sector 44, Gurgaon 122003, India

Typeset in Minion Pro 11/15.7
by InoSoft Systems Noida

Printed and bound in India
by Manipal Technologies Limited, Manipal

# CONTENTS

# INTRODUCTION

HINDI CINEMA ISN'T ABOUT PLOTS. IT'S ABOUT SUBPLOTS. Often, it's about the flashback of the prologue of a subplot, with an 'item number' thrown in if the budget can be squeezed just that bit more. The story behind the making of all of the above is quite something else and certainly does not lend itself to a linear history given the happy, alluring chaos of the Hindi film industry.

The idea for this book was to thus explore the history of Hindi cinema in a slightly chaotic way, to probe the various aspects that make it so distinctive – and tie it all into a narrative that paints a picture of the industry that has brought to millions of people a century of entertainment.

Trying to fit in a colourful century's worth of action into a 200-page book has its pitfalls. For starters, one can expect die-hard fans to be up in arms, screaming,

'Where's the chapter on directors?' 'Seriously? There's no Ranjeet in the book?' 'So many brilliant biopics and these are the ones you've come up with?' 'Where are Salman and Katrina in the chapter on pairings?' 'I mean…who let you write this book?'

But, for better or for worse, here it is – a short volume that presents ten curated lists (of ten entries each) of things peculiar to Hindi cinema, giving a picture of how the industry has evolved. In no way is this a scholarly account; it is, from the first page to the last, a fan's personal view. The chapters are guaranteed to rekindle memories. They will certainly generate passionate debates. And at least some of them will trigger in readers a desire to injure the author in some way. Nothing that a friendly banter on cinema should not provoke…

Ultimately, the idea and structure of this book is to feed its readers' love for Hindi cinema. To make them look up some of the films and stars mentioned. To play some songs once again. To remind them of the first time they watched a film, or about a film they didn't manage to watch. Because that's what Hindi cinema does – it draws you back again and again. After all, it was Hindi cinema they were talking about when they sang, '*Sau saal pehle, mujhe tumse pyar tha, aaj bhi hai aur kal bhi rahega...*'

# 1

# SABSE BADA RUPAIYA

## A HISTORY OF BOX-OFFICE COLLECTIONS

THE NUMBER OF WEEKS A FILM RUNS IN CINEMAS.

The length of the queues at advance-booking counters.

The price of tickets sold in 'black'.

The number of other new releases pushed back to keep one film centre stage.

The number of stars attending the premiere.

The number of stars in the opening reviews.

The Hindi film industry has always had very interesting indices for measuring the success of a film. Yet, nothing quite changes the fact that, in the end, it is all about the money, honey! Whatever be the measure, the real deal is always the money in the bank, what the film industry calls 'box office'.

THE first record holder of the highest box-office collections was – well – *Raja Harishchandra* (1913).

It was No. 1 in a field of one. Jokes apart, the film's collections were not a pushover, because even though more and more films had started to be made almost immediately after its release, *Raja Harishchandra* retained the top position for some time. Being a novelty – an Indian story told in moving pictures – the film travelled far and wide across India, collecting a sizeable sum. Legend has it that so much of the film's collections were in coins that most of it was sent to Bombay on bullock carts.

CINEMA was the big new thing in town. Both silent films and the talkies made a fair bit of money. However, the title of the first-ever blockbuster of Hindi cinema goes to *Kismet* (1943). It made eye-popping business of ₹1 crore when ticket prices were just a few *annas*. To put this in perspective, a superhit in today's terms makes ₹100 crore at an average ticket price of ₹100. This means about a crore tickets are sold. Assuming an average ticket price of about half a rupee in the early 1940s, *Kismet* sold two crore tickets among a much smaller population base. The film also held the record for the longest run for a Hindi film (187 weeks in Calcutta's Roxy cinema) for three decades, until *Sholay* broke it. The film's novelty lay in lead actor Ashok Kumar's character – a pickpocket and a con man, considered to be Hindi cinema's first anti-hero. The plot – centred around lost-and-found members of an extended family

– also became a template for other film-makers to follow (in a documentary on his life and work, Manmohan Desai mentions *Kismet* as the earliest 'lost-and-found' film, a genre that he subsequently made his own), while the subplot involving an unmarried mother was surprisingly progressive for the times. A key element of the film's success was the hyper-nationalistic song it featured: 'Door hato ae duniya walon, Hindustan humara hai'. That the song didn't get edited out (and its creators punished) by the ever-vigilant British censors was a wonder. At some point, the makers claimed that the words *duniya walon* in the song referred to the Axis Powers fighting the British-Indian army in the Second World War.

*Kismet* catapulted Ashok Kumar into the position of the first superstar of Hindi cinema. When director Himanshu Rai persuaded Ashok Kumar to act in the film, his salary was ₹250 per month. It increased to ₹1,000 when *Kismet* was being made. After *Kismet*, Ashok Kumar walked out of the Bombay Talkies film studio due to creative differences with Amiya Chakraborty, then head of the studio, and joined a new studio, Filmistan. Here his salary was doubled to ₹2,000 and he was also allowed to work for other studios – thus ending the rigid system followed till then, of each artiste exclusively contracted to work with one production house or studio. Soon after, he was paid an astronomical

₹1 lakh for Mehboob Khan's *Najma* (1943), and later an even more eye-popping ₹2.5 lakh for Debaki Bose's *Chandrashekhar* (1947).

As the Second World War ended, many businessmen who made their fortunes from war-time profiteering started financing films, lured by the glamour associated with the film world, and the Hindi film industry became inextricably linked to big bucks. As they say, film industry *mein sab kismet ka khel hai...* Indeed, it's all fated.

THE late 1940s brought forth the box-office phenomenon called Raj Kapoor. A born storyteller, Raj Kapoor acted in films (often very bad ones) to save up money and make the films he wanted to. Every penny he earned was invested back in his productions, which he also directed. The making of his films was always fraught with financial problems – running on loans, mortgaged properties and deferred payments to creditors. The end result, though, in his expert hands, was always quite electric – and his films attained box-office gold well before they were hailed as classics of Hindi cinema. *Barsaat* (1949) was the film that broke *Kismet*'s record in terms of collections and raked in more than a crore rupees. Yet, the film that followed *Barsaat* was even more legendary, in all senses of the term.

*Awara* (1951) was in competition for the Grand Prize at the Cannes Film Festival and received glowing reviews in India and abroad. The film had become hugely popular even before critical acclaim came along. *Awara* had collected ₹1.25 crore at the domestic box office and became the highest grosser of all time (at the time) in Hindi cinema. This was bolstered – or, rather, dwarfed – by what was Indian cinema's first major international foray – into Russia. When *Awara* released in what was still the Union of Soviet Socialist Republics (USSR) in 1954, it instantly became a phenomenon. An estimated 64 million Russians watched the film and the title song, 'Awara hoon…', was soon being hummed across the length and breadth of the country. (Incidentally, *Awara* was a huge success in China as well, and 'Awara hoon…' was one of Chairman Mao's favourite songs. When the Chinese Premier Zhou Enlai visited India, he requested the performers at his official banquet to sing the song.) *Awara* generated a revenue of approximately 29 million Soviet Rubles (at the time about ₹3.4 crore). The film's massive success in the Soviet Union probably led Raj Kapoor to doff his cap to the Russians in his next film, *Shree 420*, in the lyrics of the iconic song 'Mera joota hai Japani'.

The Soviet regime carried out cultural exchanges only with select countries. *Awara*'s success led to Hindi cinema getting a lion's share of the market for foreign films there. In later years, the Mithun Chakraborty-starrer *Disco Dancer* (1982), along with its songs, became a gigantic hit in Russia – but it had all started with *Awara*. Raj Kapoor's box-office draw continued with his 1955 release *Shree 420* also becoming the highest grosser among Hindi films till then. It also became the first Indian film to earn a domestic collection of ₹2 crore.

THE film that broke the ₹1–₹2 crore range of box-office collections (which several films did in the middle years of the 1950s) was iconic in every way possible.

Mehboob Khan was known to be a producer–director of grand spectacles. He made *Aan* (1952), which was briefly the biggest hit of Hindi cinema till *Shree 420* overtook it. In 1957, he produced and directed *Mother India*, a film that created new benchmarks for Indian cinema. It was an expensive film – probably the most expensive till then – which was mounted lavishly, used a massive numbers of extras and props, and shot in a variety of locations.

The collections from *Mother India* were spectacular too. It is estimated that the film collected ₹4 crore in the domestic box office – the highest at the time by a long margin. This obviously didn't include the money made by scalpers selling tickets in 'black' because both Mehboob Khan and Nargis had a huge following by then. This aspect of the film was immortalized in *Kala Bazar* (1960), in which Dev Anand is shown to be selling tickets of *Mother India* on the 'black market' at hugely inflated prices as the film's premiere plays in the background.

The film also reached USSR and other countries of the Eastern Bloc, South America and the Middle East – earning a tidy sum from these places as well. It was India's entry to the Academy Awards for Best Foreign Language Film in 1958. *Mother India* was nominated to the final five but lost out to Federico Fellini's *Nights of Cabiria*. A good run of the film in the Americas or a win at the Academy Awards could have set Indian cinema on an international trajectory, but even without that achievement *Mother India* remains a landmark film that distinguished Hindi cinema from the rest.

AS far as landmark films go – marked by a wide canvas, huge sets, grand locations, elaborate costumes, great stars – it all came together in perfect symphony in K. Asif's *Mughal-e-Azam* (1960). At a time when films were shot within budgets of ₹15–₹25 lakh on an average, the expenditure for making *Mughal-e-Azam* was a whopping ₹1.5 crore – making it the most expensive film produced in India till then. The financier of such a gigantic film had to have come from outside the film industry, and in this case it was Pallonji Shapoorji Mistry. A construction tycoon and the holder of the highest number of shares of Tata Sons, Mistry came on board in 1951 and hung on (despite differences with the director and frequent budget escalations) till the film was completed in 1960.

The film opened in Maratha Mandir in August 1960. It was rumoured that a crowd of more than one lakh people had landed up when the advance bookings opened. The distributors seemed to be in sync with the audience's expectations as rights for distribution territories in the country were sold for as high as ₹17 lakh. This was at a time when the norm was in the range of ₹3–₹4 lakh. Effectively, everyone associated with the film bet their reputations (or their last shirt) on it. When such things happen in real life, people begin to predict the onset of doomsday. (And when people bet their last shirt on something, they usually lose it.) This is where *Mughal-e-Azam* turned out to be as much of a fairy tale in real life as it was in its reel existence. The film collected an estimated ₹5.5 crore at the domestic box office, nearly four times its astronomical production budget. This was possibly because it was released in 150 theatres simultaneously, which was unheard of in those days. The one lakh crazies who landed up for the advance booking probably ended up watching the film – many of them multiple times – at ticket prices that were inflated just for the film. Maratha Mandir, where *Mughal-e-Azam* premiered, continued to show the film for the next six years to packed houses.[1] The records it set in its collections and its run were not to be broken in a hurry.

WHEN I say 'not in a hurry', I really mean it. For the film that broke *Mughal-e-Azam*'s record came exactly 15 years and 10 days after the release of the original record smasher. Ballooning budgets, a grand spectacle, a legendary star cast and high repeat value for audiences were common to both films. And, like its illustrious predecessor, the later film also broke every doomsday prediction that was made about it.

*Sholay* (1975), the film that did this, started with a planned budget of ₹1 crore, a massive sum in the 1970s, but during the course of the filming – in which director Ramesh Sippy and producer G.P. Sippy spared literally no expense to mount 'the greatest story ever told' – it increased to ₹3 crore. The amount was so large that the film industry seemed to give up on the hope that the film would ever recover its costs, let alone turn in a profit. However, G.P. Sippy was a gambler like no other. He backed the huge production budget with a significant marketing budget and advertised the film for several weeks in trade magazines and major cities

[1] Maratha Mandir has a penchant for long-running records. In 1995, it started showing a film that continued to be shown till 1,000 weeks later. That film was *Dilwale Dulhania Le Jayenge*.

to draw in audiences. This had not been done for any other film of the time.

*Sholay*'s reception was muted in the trade and the press. It is often said that *Sholay* 'flopped' in its initial days, but that was probably a result of trade reports that predicted the film wouldn't recover its costs despite a good collection, simply because the costs were way too high. The Sippys panicked enough to seriously contemplate going back to their shooting location and reshooting the ending of the film. Amitabh Bachchan had become a huge star post the release of *Deewaar* earlier that year and for a while they thought that keeping his character alive would perhaps improve the film's prospects.

At this point, two things happened that changed the narrative in the trade while also highlighting the impact of the film on the audience. The writers of the film – Salim Khan and Javed Akhtar – supremely confident of their script, published an ad in the trade papers. At a time when the pundits were predicting that the film would earn a revenue of ₹40 lakh per distribution territory, Salim–Javed announced in the ad that *Sholay* would do business of ₹1 crore per territory. Ramesh Sippy too was told by a theatre owner that he knew the film had tremendous impact because not one person in the audience was leaving the theatre during the interval.

For the Sippys, who were fearing financial ruin, these were much-needed shots in the arm.

Well, *Sholay* prevailed. And how.

It completed its silver jubilee (25 weeks running in cinemas) in more than 100 theatres and its golden jubilee (50 weeks in cinemas) in 60 – a record that has not been broken yet and is unlikely to be broken ever again. It ran for five years at Bombay's Minerva Theatre – to the point that the bus stop opposite the theatre came to be called the '*Sholay* stop'. The film is supposed to have made a net domestic collection of ₹15 crore, nearly three times the collection of the previous record-holder. In terms of box-office revenue, re-release rights and music rights, *Sholay* set benchmarks and revealed to the industry revenue streams that didn't exist earlier. Distributors, exhibitors, black-marketers – everyone made a tonne of money on the film.

*SHOLAY'S* was not a record to be broken – and yet it was, by a film that changed the way the box-office game was played in India. The 1980s were one of the least creative decades in Hindi cinema. Formulaic plots largely derivative of the films made in the 1970s ruled the roost. The films were marked by a profusion of sex and violence that kept family audiences away. The home video segment was booming and people were watching films on video-cassette players, fast-forwarding through songs and watching copy-paste heroes fight cardboard villains in cut-price sets on a 21-inch screen.

This changed with *Hum Aapke Hain Koun..!* (1994), Sooraj Barjatya's big-budget offering after the unexpected monster success of *Maine Pyar Kiya* (1989). Rajshri Productions, the group that produced the film, and a well-known film distributor as well, had a strategy of releasing its films in a small number of theatres, and slowly increasing the number of prints and theatres as the film became successful. To make this strategy a success, Rajshri Productions didn't release the film on video. This was a big risk and a radical departure from the prevailing norm. Given the company's equity after *Maine Pyar Kiya*, film exhibitors were doubly keen to bag its next production right from the beginning. The owners of the group, the Barjatyas, handpicked the exhibitors for the film and restricted its release only to those who had upgraded their theatres for optimal viewing and made the facilities suitable for family audiences. This led to a trend-defying phenomenon of families coming back to theatres, despite the steep increase in ticket prices that necessarily followed the upgrades. The familiar, endearing story of the film made audiences feel like it was an extended family wedding and crowds began flocking to the cinema all over again.

It is easy to say that *Hum Aapke Hain Koun..!* was a blockbuster because it collected an astounding ₹72 crore at the domestic box-office when the previous record was about ₹15 crore. But it did much more than that. By bringing back audiences to the theatres, increasing the average price of tickets and forcing the industry to give audiences a proper cinema-viewing experience, it made revenue-generation easier for forthcoming films. A trade website, BoxOfficeIndia.com, notes that after *Hum Aapke Hain Koun..!*, the qualifier for what made a blockbuster no longer remained a collection of ₹10 crore – it became ₹20 crore. In short, it raised the bar to an unprecedented level.

It needs to be said here that in the five years prior to the film, 1989 to 1993, the biggest hits of the years collected an average of ₹12.2 crore. In the subsequent five years, 1995 to 1999, the biggest hits collected an average of ₹44.2 crore. Effectively, within a decade, the film pushed up the revenue by a factor of four.

THE new millennium brought with it newer directions for Hindi films. The year 2001 saw an Indian film shortlisted in the Oscar Awards in the Best Foreign Language Film category. The film was *Lagaan*. That year, audiences also watched a film that is widely considered to have made Hindi films 'cool' – *Dil Chahta Hai* – and a film that is still considered to be a casting coup with three megastars from three generations – *Kabhi Khushi*

*Kabhie Gham*. Yet, the film that 'uprooted' these films to become the highest grosser of the year was big enough to beat even *Hum Aapke Hain Koun..!* It was a love story, but unlike any that audiences of Hindi films had ever watched before.

*Gadar: Ek Prem Katha* came at a time when multiplexes were beginning to sprout and ticket prices had inflated considerably. Film-makers were also starting to realize that urban audiences were enough to rake in the money that would make a film a hit, and the industry saw film-makers making a distinct shift to reach that audience. *Gadar*, however, concentrated on its hero Sunny Deol's constituency. Punjab, Haryana, Delhi and other parts of northern India were where the film did maximum business – generating far higher footfalls to earn the collections it did. In fact, BoxOfficeIndia.com estimates that *Gadar* garnered one of the highest footfalls among all Hindi films that came before it.

*Gadar* made a net domestic collection of ₹77 crore, large parts of it from non-metro audiences, and if one goes by the list of top grossers of the first two decades of the new millennium one can safely say that *Gadar* was probably the last film to do so.

IN the 2000s, the race to the top involved a large number of contenders. Think about it this way: from 1943 to 2001 there were nine films that broke records to become the top grossers (all of which are listed above). From 2002 onwards, up to 2017, six films have already broken successive records. Gone are the days when a film remained the top grosser for years on end the way *Mughal-e-Azam* (15 years), *Sholay* (19 years) or even *Hum Aapke Hain Koun..!* (7 years) did. In this crowded race, it is probably better to look at films in clusters instead of as individual record-holders.

*Ghajini*, which released in 2008, is important primarily because it was the first film to hit domestic box-office collections of ₹100 crore and thus create a lasting benchmark. For years, the Hindi film industry had been obsessed with time. The success of films was measured by the duration for which they ran in theatres. Their staying power had a direct correlation with the revenue they collected, but the real currency was the number of 'jubilees' they celebrated. (Filmstar Rajendra Kumar was nicknamed Jubilee Kumar for the succession of jubilee hits he starred in!) In this scenario, *Ghajini* collected more than ₹100 crore (₹114 crore, to be precise) and started the 100-Crore Club.

BEFORE we move to the next record-breaking 'club', we must take a quick detour to visit another phenomenon of box-office success: a franchise.

In the same way that Hollywood studios create franchises out of superheroes, sets of characters and even themes, the biggest Hindi film studio of the present started one with *Dhoom* (2004) – a decent hit in India and abroad – which presented John Abraham, who had until then played the clean 'hero', with a dark twist. This seemingly common twist was amped up in *Dhoom 2* (2006), in which Hrithik Roshan played the villain, and the film became the biggest domestic grosser of all time (collecting ₹81 crore and overtaking *Gadar*). And that wasn't all. Its third instalment (which released in 2013) had Aamir Khan playing the bad guy and it became the highest grosser of all time (at ₹260 crore), beating another Aamir Khan-starrer (*3 Idiots*) in the process.

This franchise formula of a cast packed with stars, a story brimming with pulsating action, its spectacular mounting and the relentless marketing and promotional activities surrounding its launch irked the critics with its weak script, but the glamour-hungry audience lapped it up just as well. The *Dhoom* franchise started a saga of sequels in Hindi cinema, in which only a tenuous link of themes (not necessarily stories or characters) held subsequent films together after the first became a hit.

THIS brings us to the last set of films, also connected by Aamir Khan, perfectionist actor and box-office god rolled into one.

When *Ghajini* started the 100-Crore Club in 2008, no one expected the formation of a 200-Crore Club in the very next year, but Aamir Khan did just that with *3 Idiots*. Buoyed by the magic touch of Rajkumar Hirani, the film packed in a relevant message alongside superb entertainment. In fact, this was Hirani's hallmark from his earlier Munna Bhai films. The Hirani–Khan duo – in fact, the Hirani–Khan–Chopra trio, if you include producer Vidhu Vinod Chopra – performed an out-of-this-world trick. They created the 300-Crore Club with *PK* (2014), which went on to collect ₹338 crore at the domestic box-office while dispensing cautionary advice about organized religion and its purveyors. But Aamir Khan wasn't done yet. Less than two years later, he starred in the Nitesh Tiwari-directed *Dangal* and almost kicked off the 400-Crore Club at the domestic box office. It is to Aamir Khan's credit that he created these records with outstanding films, all of them delivering an important social message and living up to the exalted aims of cinema – to simultaneously educate and entertain its audience.

While hitting these milestones in India, Aamir Khan has also created an almost absurdly strong franchise in China of all places. What fuelled his popularity in our formidable neighbouring country was *Taare Zameen Par* (2007), but it soon transformed into a fandom, and by the time *Dangal* hit the Chinese theatres (9000 screens, actually) Aamir Khan had become a craze. Talk-show appearances, fan clubs, merchandise, tribute videos and all other paraphernalia combined to give *Dangal* an estimated box-office collection of $185 million (yes, that's about ₹1,200 crore). That *Dangal* has gone on to collect about ₹2,000 crore worldwide is almost incidental to the fact that it has helped Hindi cinema open up a market in China, and several films have released there in between the making of *3 Idiots* and *Dangal*. (For those who are a tad more curious, for co-producer Disney Studios, *Dangal* was their fourth-largest worldwide grosser of 2017. *Guardians of the Galaxy Vol. 2*, *Pirates of the Caribbean 5* and *The Beauty and the Beast* were followed by the adventures of the Phogat sisters!)

This is what truly successful films do. Perhaps more than creating records (which will get broken sooner or later), they create new markets, initiate new ways of doing business, and inspire new ways of making and marketing films.

## Ten films dubbed in Hindi (not necessarily the biggest hits)

***Baahubali: The Beginning*** and ***Baahubali 2*** (Telugu, 2015 and 2017): S.S. Rajamouli's double-barrelled tales of valour with astounding VFX effects were released in so many languages that one can never be sure of what (and how many) records they broke, but they were the highest-grossing films dubbed into Hindi from a south Indian language.

***Enthiran AKA Robot*** (Tamil, 2010): A Rajnikanth film (of course!) was the previous record holder. The cherry on the cake for this film was Srinivas Menon's special effects, directed by the visionary Shankar.

***The Jungle Book*** (English, 2016): Buoyed by nostalgia of the 1990s television series (and Gulzar–Vishal Bhardwaj's iconic jingle 'Jungle jungle pata chala hai, chaddi pehen ke phool khila hai'), this Hollywood remake of the 1967 Disney animated feature became the highest-grossing film of all times among English films dubbed in Hindi.

***Avatar*** (English, 2009): The euphoria over the world's biggest box-office hit (at the time) percolated down to Hindi-film audiences and the dubbed version made a tonne of money.

***Furious 7*** (English, 2015): This particular instalment of the series hit new highs at the box office, although it was unfortunate that its success was mainly attributed to the tragic death of the franchise's lead, Paul Walker, while the film was in the making.

***2012*** (English, 2009): The disaster film about the world coming to an end struck a chord among Indian viewers. People probably saw shades of their rush-hour traffic in the film!

***Spiderman 3*** (English, 2007): One of the earliest superhero films to find a major audience in Hindi, it ensured that the producers of such films focus on the Hindi film market.

***Indra the Tiger*** (Telugu, 2002): This Chiranjeevi-starrer, blockbuster film is an unlikely but deserving candidate on this list for being one of the most watched dubbed films on Indian television.

***Jurassic Park*** (English, 1993): A game-changer as far as Hollywood is concerned, the Spielberg classic launched with 100+ prints in India, nearly 80 per cent of which were in Indian languages.

***Roja*** (Tamil, 1992): The Hindi version of this film turned A.R. Rahman into a national star and even the stilted lyrics of the Hindi songs could not stifle the magical experience of the music.

# 2

# JODI NO. 1

## A HISTORY OF CHEMISTRY

THAT THE HINDI FILM INDUSTRY IS DIFFERENT FROM all its counterparts becomes evident when you watch the award shows. While every other film award function ends with the two most important awards – Best Director and Best Film – ours ends with the two most important to us – Best Actor and Best Actress. With everything that Hindi films entail – the beautifully picturized songs (and dances), lovingly crafted dialogues and the dramatic play of emotions – we cannot do without placing all our love (and money) at the feet of our stars. Suffice it to say that different stages of evolution of the industry have been defined not by directors or producers, but by 'hit' pairs of heroines and heroes.

**Ashok Kumar and Devika Rani**

If not for anything else, the pairing of Ashok Kumar

and Devika Rani on screen should be remembered for being probably the only one in the history of Hindi cinema in which the woman was older than the man. (Given how quickly our heroines fall out of public favour – and how long our heroes hang on – this was quite something.) Their pairing started with a most scandalous episode – all of it Devika Rani's doing. She had run off with the handsome male lead of the film she was shooting for and had to be persuaded by her boss to return to the studio. Her beau was quietly let go, and the aforementioned boss plucked out a Bengali technical assistant from the labs (whose work had sufficiently impressed him on a previous occasion) and paired her with him. Did I mention that the boss was also her husband? Well, now I have!

Their first pairing was in *Jeevan Naiya* (1936), which was moderately successful and paved the way for *Achhut Kanya* (1936). All the templates from which early black-and-white Hindi films – the sing-song style of dialogue delivery, the nasal singing, the overly innocent romantic situations – pretty much derived from the second film and continue to be recognizable to this day. The film struck a chord with its story about untouchables, some smashing music and a fresh lead pair and went on to become a massive hit – massive enough for the lead pair to be cast in quick succession in around seven films in the span of a couple of years.

Several decades later, it is difficult to fathom which aspect of the film clicked with the audience. Devika Rani had an elfin charm and the confidence of a major star. Ashok Kumar clearly didn't yet have the panache that he exuded in some of his later roles, even as a character actor. Their chemistry was awkward and there are enough stories about Ashok Kumar's reluctance to become an actor and his callow behaviour during shooting. But, despite all that, Ashok Kumar and Devika Rani's combination was hugely successful and laid the foundation for the studio – Bombay Talkies – becoming a film-making behemoth. In a way, their success turned the balance of power in Indian cinema towards Bombay. There were other film-making centres in India at the time (like Calcutta and Pune, among others) but a slew of successes from Bombay Talkies improved the studio's equity manifold and many key actors and technicians gravitated to what was now considered the No. 1 studio in India.

In a way, Ashok Kumar and Devika Rani continued their partnership even when they were not acting opposite each other – he as a superstar actor and she as the producer, that is, the owner of Bombay Talkies after her husband Himanshu Rai's death. Bombay Talkies had a good run under Devika Rani, producing many films starring a much-improved Ashok Kumar himself, till about 1943, when prolific producer Sashadhar

Mukherjee, Ashok Kumar and several others left the studio to form Filmistan Studio, and Bombay Talkies no longer remained the prime mover in the Hindi film industry.

**Raj Kapoor and Nargis**

Around this time, a second-generation actor was starting to build on his dreams of owning a studio, and R.K. Films was born. The most identifiable part of the studio – its logo – was the result of the owner's sizzling chemistry with his most famous lead actress. Raj Kapoor was paying a senior producer, Jaddan Bai, a courtesy visit when her daughter opened the door. They both took a moment to admire each other's deadly good looks and clicked from the word go. (Raj Kapoor and Nargis's first meeting has been immortalized in *Bobby* [1973], in the scene where Rishi Kapoor meets Dimple Kapadia for the first time. She pushes back her hair with besan-smeared hands, leaving besan batter in her hair.)

The two actors had an almost animal magnetism that manifested in iconic scenes in innumerable films, most notably in *Barsaat*, *Awara* and *Shree 420*. Each of these films shows a woman clearly devoted to her man, suffering his tantrums and cruelty. This has often been described as the 'caveman concept of love' which involves an educated, financially self-sufficient woman behaving subserviently with a man. But Nargis's characters also embodied the moral beacon to which the wayward Raj – also the name of his character in many of the films – returned for redemption and solace. This symbolism was brought alive almost literally in the last scene of their last film together. At the end of *Jagte Raho* (1956), Raj Kapoor's character is revived when he drinks water poured into his cupped hands by Nargis's character, the mother figure. This is interesting because Raj Kapoor called Nargis 'the mother of my films' (just as his wife was the mother of his children).

Raj Kapoor and Nargis acted in a large number of films together. The rift between them came about when Nargis refused to play an older woman in a proposed R.K. film, but agreed to play the part of a mother with grown-up sons in *Mother India*. Their personal relationship too seemed to be going nowhere, despite Nargis's every effort. (It was said that she even appealed to the then chief minister of Bombay State, Morarji Desai, to find a way for her to marry Raj Kapoor.) The duo eventually stopped acting together, ended their relationship as Nargis married Sunil Dutt, and the two stars went their separate ways. Nargis never stepped into R.K. Studios again – till she was invited years later for Rishi Kapoor's wedding. The story goes that at the ceremony the potential awkwardness that could have occurred between Indian cinema's best-matched couple was smoothed over by Raj Kapoor's gracious wife, and the two stars – and their families – remained on good terms after that.

**Dilip Kumar and Madhubala**

The question of whether off-screen chemistry translates into on-screen chemistry brings us to a couple whose on-screen presence couldn't be more radically different from each other. Dilip Kumar's brooding intensity was a terrific counterpoint to Madhubala's sparkling effervescence. Dilip Kumar wrote in his memoirs that 'she was sprightly and vivacious, and she could draw me out of my shyness and reticence effortlessly.'

Dilip Kumar and Madhubala were both discovered by Devika Rani – yes, she's more important to Hindi cinema than you think – and launched by Bombay Talkies. (Incidentally, Devika Rani renamed them too! Yusuf Khan and Begum Mumtaz Jahan Dehlavi were given caste-agnostic Hindu names to maximize their appeal in post-Partition India.) When they first worked together, both of them were already stars in their own right. They looked extremely good on screen, complemented each other's styles of acting and fell in love with each other for good measure. Their impact as a couple was far greater than the four films they did together. When Dilip Kumar proposed marriage to her, their pairing generated massive interest and the then forthcoming *Mughal-e-Azam* looked all set to become the first of many landmarks they'd create as a couple. But what they say about good times not lasting came true when Madhubala's overly possessive father, in Dilip Kumar's own words, 'attempted to make the proposed marriage into a business venture'. The love story – in true filmi fashion – got derailed due to paternal interference and unfortunately – unlike filmi stories – did not have a happy ending.

Their relationship was so strained that when they shot for the famous scene in *Mughal-e-Azam* in which Salim caresses Anarkali with a feather they were not even on speaking terms. After that, the situation worsened when the producers of their film *Naya Daur* (1957) sued Madhubala for refusing to travel for an outdoor shoot. In the best tradition of climaxes in Hindi cinema, Dilip Kumar appeared in court to testify for the producers, but ended up expressing his love for Madhubala. 'I, too, loved her,' he said, before admitting that they would not be getting married due to her responsibilities to her family.

Then they walked into the sunset. Separately. Breaking more hearts than just their own.

**Guru Dutt and Waheeda Rehman**

When it came to walking into a (somewhat muted) sunset, no one (and no pair) could beat Guru Dutt and

Waheeda Rehman. Be it the poet and the prostitute walking into the fog (*Pyaasa*, 1957) or the director and the filmstar getting separated by success (*Kaagaz Ke Phool*, 1959), even their unions had a shadow of an ending looming over them (sometimes even of death, as in *Chaudhvin Ka Chand* [1960] and *Sahib Bibi Aur Ghulam* [1962]).

Guru Dutt was the perennial outsider and Waheeda Rehman his muse. It seems apt that they first met outside the world of Hindi cinema, in Hyderabad, where Guru Dutt and Abrar Alvi had gone to buy rights for a Telugu film. The two ended up meeting Waheeda Rehman instead. She had become hugely popular on the back of a dance number she performed in a Telugu film and had come to meet someone in the same distributor's office where they were waiting. In his biography, Alvi claims that they were just about impressed by the young actress but she had obviously made an impact because Guru Dutt remembered her much later (when they were shooting for *CID* which released in 1956) and signed her on for three years. Despite being a newcomer, Waheeda Rehman had specific demands: She refused to change her name; and she was aloof during shoots and rehearsals. That the arrangement was retained despite this is an indication of the support she had from her boss.

The reclusive actor–director ended up playing

pensive, introverted characters in films as well and Waheeda Rehman was the solace he needed. Their relationship caused a lot of strife in Guru Dutt's personal life but he continued with it nevertheless. It was only when Geeta Dutt, his wife, had an affair, that Guru Dutt ended his relationship with Rehman. Whether this was a result of the realization of the emotional trauma he had caused his wife or of his ego being wounded is a matter of conjecture. The ending of this relationship, too, was coloured by all the drama and melodrama of our cinema, with Waheeda Rehman even being stopped from using the make-up rooms she was accustomed to. In *Kaagaz Ke Phool*, the failed director is shown walking out of the studio, his star protégé following close behind. In real life, the protégé was unceremoniously ejected from the studio and the director lived with the guilt of having been the instrument of her ouster till he could no longer do so. Guru Dutt's death from an overdose of sleeping pills and alcohol has been called both a suicide and an accident. Whichever it may have been, he was at the time in an extremely fragile state of mind – separated from his muse and not fully reconciled with his wife.

**Rajesh Khanna and Sharmila Tagore**

Not all the crackling on-screen chemistry spills off-screen. Some actors just remain good friends. No, really, they do! The pivotal moment of Rajesh Khanna and

Sharmila Tagore's partnership comes halfway into their first film together – *Aradhana* – when Rajesh Khanna in his second role in the film walks across an airport tarmac and meets Sharmila Tagore, his onscreen mother. Less than one hour of screen-time earlier, the pair were in love, but now they seem absolutely believable as a mother–son pair. Sharmila herself explained the unique chemistry the two shared. 'He had a vulnerable, lost air about him that made women of all ages feel very protective,' she said in the foreword of a biography of Rajesh Khanna and, indeed, their most famous films together had the two playing characters across the widest range of ages, emotional states and even looks. In *Safar* (1970), they were in a relationship doomed by a terminal disease. In *Amar Prem* (1972), their unrequited love story was spread over decades. In *Daag* (1973), they were in entangled in a three-way relationship. In *Aavishkar* (1974), they were a couple going through the ups and downs of married life.

Rajesh Khanna had several hit pairings in his dream run as a superstar and his pairing with Mumtaz was probably the most successful, but the way Sharmila Tagore balanced his youthful intensity with the sensuality of a lover and the serenity of an older woman was something unique. After his death, Sharmila Tagore wrote an affectionate obituary alluding to the roles that made them both legendary. Remembering the dashing pilot from *Aradhana* (1969), she signed off with: 'Goodbye, Flight Lieutenant Arun. I'll miss you. We all will.'

**Dharmendra and Hema Malini**

If Rajesh–Sharmila played the unconventional couple onscreen, Dharmendra and Hema Malini constituted the quintessential Hindi-film couple – probably the best matched in terms of looks, popularity and the joie de vivre they exuded. This played out in the longevity of their popularity. While most star pairs lasted, at best, a decade, Dharmendra and Hema Malini's last film as lead pair released 17 years after their first and they have acted in nearly thirty films together.

In the 1970s, the two of them were an extremely powerful box-office draw – matching up to the star power of even Amitabh Bachchan at his peak. Be it *Seeta aur Geeta* (1972), *Sholay*, *Chacha Bhatija* (1977), *Jugnu* (1973), *Raja Jani* (1972) or even a relative failure like *Razia Sultan* (1983), Garam Dharam and the Dream Girl exemplified filmi masala. Playing standard tropes of the dashing, heart-of-gold hero and the buxom, chirpy heroine who never stops talking, they didn't break fresh ground in terms of characterization but churned out hit after hit. If there is a strike rate of hits among star couples, theirs is likely to be the highest.

However, their real-life love story is probably more dramatic than their films. The much-married Dharmendra bribing spot boys to goof up with the lighting so that he could do multiple takes of embracing Hema is the stuff of filmi lore (documented to have happened on the sets of *Sholay*, and it probably occurred on other film sets too!). The romance culminated in a dramatic wedding between Dilawar Khan and Aisha Bi, when they converted to Islam so that they could marry without Dharmendra having to divorce his first wife.

**Dev Anand and Zeenat Aman**

Hindi cinema is notorious for alarming mismatches when it comes to pairing of lead players separated in age by decades and this casting anomaly was elevated almost to an art form by the legendary Dev Anand. In 1971, he launched Zeenat Aman in *Hare Rama Hare Krishna* though they played siblings in the film. The similarly-aged on-screen siblings were played by actors who were about thirty years apart in biological age. The massive success of *Hare Rama Hare Krishna* led, almost immediately, to their romantic pairing and they played the Bohemian couple in style in film after film. Be it the progressive author and his fan in *Prem Shastra* (1974), the diamond-chasers in *Heera Panna* (1973), the on-the-run convicts in *Warrant* (1975), or the circus acrobats in *Kalabaaz* (1977), Dev Anand and Zeenat

Aman always brought a touch of the exotic to their roles. The age difference was fairly apparent - Zeenat was truly a with-it woman of the times while Dev Anand tried his best to catch up. Given Dev Anand's stubborn refusal to play non-lead roles, their partnership in a way institutionalized the May–December pairings in Hindi cinema. The pairing was successful but lasted for a short, breathless burst, with romantic investment from Dev Anand's side at least. However, the partnership ended when Raj Kapoor signed Zeenat Aman for *Satyam Shivam Sundaram* (1978). Dev Anand became suspicious that the two were getting romantically involved and thereafter quickly moved on to launching other heroines.

**Amitabh Bachchan and Rekha**

Gossip about a star pair's romantic involvement has always accompanied their professional success but never was it as aggressive as with Amitabh Bachchan and Rekha. In the 1970s a slew of gossip magazines focusing on the Hindi film industry were in circulation - the most notable among these being *Stardust* - and in retaliation to Bachchan's boycott of the press, the coverage was as vicious as it was relentless. *Stardust* introduced a deliberately gossipy (read bitchy) tone to their coverage of industry gossip and other magazines gleefully joined in. Bachchan - it was believed in the press – used his clout with the then ruling family of the country to gag some of the publications and became, therefore, a more frequent target.

In line with Bachchan's slow start in the industry, the first film in which Amitabh and Rekha were to be cast opposite each other saw him getting replaced by Sanjay Khan (*Duniya Kya Jaane*, 1971). Earlier, they were both cast in Hrishikesh Mukherjee's *Namak Haraam* (1973) but didn't act opposite each other and had only one scene together. One day after the release of Bachchan-starrer *Deewaar*, they started shooting for *Do Anjaane*, which was their first film as a pair – and there was no looking back after that. As the hits piled up – *Kasme Vaade*, *Muqaddar ka Sikandar* and *Ganga ki Saugandh* (all released in 1978), and *Suhaag* and *Mr Natwarlal* (both released in 1979) – so did the gossip. Prior to her pairing with Bachchan, Rekha was a casual actress – not overly interested in her looks or performance. But, as she worked with him, she became a hardworking style icon. Both of them were extremely well-spoken and their dialogues entered a different dimension in romantic scenes. In an explosive interview published in *Stardust* in 1978 , Rekha claimed that at the trial show for *Muqaddar ka Sikandar*, Jaya Bachchan was saddened to tears while watching their on-screen chemistry. Apparently, Bachchan stopped acting with her after this (ostensibly to maintain peace at home) but that theory was blown away by the last film in which they acted together – *Silsila* (1981). Widely billed as the casting coup of the century, the overall film was disappointing, but it managed to brilliantly showcase the extremely potent romantic pairing of Amitabh and Rekha.

After *Silsila*, Rekha has 'appeared' with Amitabh through her voice, (by dubbing for actresses acting opposite him, most notably in *Aakhree Raasta* [1986] and *Sooryavansham* [1999]). And, of course, their legend lives on because we are yet to watch a film awards function in which Bachchan wins a prize and the cameras don't turn to Rekha.

**Shah Rukh Khan and Kajol**

If there is a pair made for awards functions and cameras, it is the contemporary duo of Shah Rukh Khan (SRK) and Kajol. It seems a little odd to use 'contemporary' to describe a couple who started appearing together more than two decades back, but their longevity as a pair has been extended by their sparkling media presence over the years.

SRK and Kajol's chemistry and appeal lay in the zone of 'sanskari modernity'. They holidayed in Europe but didn't forget the morning bhajan (*Dilwale Dulhania Le Jayenge*, 1995). They attended a college straight out of *Riverdale* (*Kuch Kuch Hota Hai*, 1998) but changed into Indian finery as soon as the occasion demanded. In their first film together (*Baazigar*, 1993), they played modern characters – but with traditional underpinnings. SRK's character was a psychopath who threw his innocent girlfriend (played by Shilpa Shetty) off a high-rise in the process of avenging his family's ruin. Kajol (playing Shilpa's sister) plunged into investigating the murder in order to fulfil her sisterly duty. The fine balance they struck between being traditional and next-gen found an excited-to-the-point-of-delirious audience among the Indian diaspora and opened up the non-resident Indian (NRI) market to Hindi films like never before. For NRIs living in foreign lands and trying to stay connected to Indian culture, the nattily dressed with-it duo reciting their daily prayers was a sight for sore eyes. Their easy chemistry seemed almost natural, given their instinctive acting styles. It helped that they had very similar world views, were very good friends (until recently, when competing films produced by SRK and Kajol's husband Ajay Devgn clashed at the box office and caused a rift), were at similar stages of their careers – moving towards superstardom almost simultaneously. Their close circle of film-maker friends and associates claimed that they were lucky charms for each other. Kajol, for example, almost stopped working in external productions in the initial years of her marriage but did guest appearances in SRK films like *Kal Ho Naa Ho* (2003), *Om Shanti Om* (2007), *Kabhi Alvida Naa Kehna* (2006) and *Rab*

*Ne Bana Di Jodi* (2008) (before, of course, teaming up again as a lead pair in *My Name Is Khan* [2010] and the more recent *Dilwale* [2015]).

**Govinda and Karisma Kapoor**

While we have observed the chemistry of lead pairs in films down the ages, Govinda and Karisma Kapoor, it could be said, dabbled more in the laws of physics than chemistry. They changed the anatomy of the Hindi film song-and-dance number by injecting a manic energy into it. That they were both exceptionally good dancers certainly helped; what helped even more were the earthy lyrics, even earthier plots and the earthiest presence of David Dhawan in the mix. Between the three of them, they changed the level of craziness that had so far marked Hindi cinema.

Govinda and Karisma's story cannot be recounted without mentioning David Dhawan, who was responsible for their biggest hits and signature style. The three of them had some industry connections, but were determined to make it on their own. Govinda's father, a small-time actor, Dhawan's filmi brothers and Karisma's *khaandaan*'s considerable clout notwithstanding, they had a hunger to prove themselves in an increasingly competitive industry.

Their films such as *Raja Babu* (1994), *Coolie No. 1* (1995), *Hero No. 1* (1997), *Saajan Chale Sasural* (1996) had songs replete with double-entendre, innuendo, exuberant dance numbers and crazier-than-crazy plots – going totally against the grain of Hindi cinema as it was known until then. Taking a route in the opposite direction to that of SRK and Kajol, Govinda and Karisma found their mojo by dismantling the sweet, thoughtful notion of filmi love and incorporating a flavour of zany raunchiness into it. They were both ridiculed for their garish costumes as well as their pelvis-thrusting dance steps, but that did nothing to stop the juggernaut they unleashed, which ran for the better part of the 1990s. By the time Karisma branched out to the 'sophisticated' side with *Dil To Pagal Hai* (1997), the partnership had reached its sell-by date. But the spirit of Govinda and Karisma live on in today's stars such as Ranveer Singh and Varun Dhawan, who grew up in the 1990s and consider the Govinda–Karisma duo to be the 'jodi no. 1'. (Although, quite unjustifiably as *Jodi No. 1* [2001] starred Sanjay Dutt, Twinkle Khanna and Monica Bedi along with Govinda!)

## Ten hit pairs deserve ten more!

**Shammi Kapoor–Asha Parekh** acted together in a number of films that exemplified the 1960s romance marked by catchy songs, parental opposition and beautiful locales. Best known for *Dil Deke Dekho* and *Teesri Manzil*.

**Dara Singh–Mumtaz** were the darlings of B-grade cinema with the muscular hero and buxom heroine complementing each other perfectly. Best known for titles involving characters such as Tarzan, Hercules and Samson!

**Sanjeev Kumar–Jaya Bhaduri** played an awesome range of roles – lovers (*Anamika*), husband–wife (*Koshish*), father–daughter (*Parichay*) and even father-in-law–daughter-in-law (*Sholay*).

**Rishi Kapoor–Neetu Singh** were Hindi cinema's best-matched pair, who kept teen romance alive in the time of action heroes. Best known for *Khel Khel Mein* (in their youth) and *Do Dooni Chaar* (in their advanced years).

**Ajit–Bindu** were the villain-moll pair who reached cult status for their Boss-Mona routine. Best known for *Zanjeer*, where they played worthy adversaries to Amitabh Bachchan's angry-young-man persona.

**Jeetendra–Sridevi/Jayaprada** ruled the 1980s with their version of romantic films that were peppered with acrobatically choreographed songs. Best known for *Tohfa*, which starred both heroines.

**Naseeruddin Shah–Shabana Azmi**, both art-house legends, delivered some of the greatest acting performances of Hindi cinema. Best known for *Masoom*, *Sparsh* and *Paar*. (Both of them won national awards for their performance in the last.)

**Om Puri–Smita Patil** are known for their searing intensity in classics of Hindi cinema like *Ardh Satya*, *Sadgati* and *Aakrosh*.

**Anil Kapoor–Madhuri Dixit**, paired in the classic mould of hero-heroine, they delivered a string of super-hits in the late 1980s and early 1990s. Best known for *Tezaab*, *Parinda* and *Ram Lakhan*.

**Akshay Kumar–Raveena Tandon** had a short and intense partnership on-screen (and apparently off-screen). Best known for *Mohra*.

# 3

# KISSA KAHAANI KA

## THE STORIES BEHIND THE STORIES

HINDI FILMS HAVE THRIVED ON THE STRANGEST methods of sourcing stories. Stories have been picked up from mythology, popular novels, previously released films in a range of languages, and even created on a hero's whim. Screenplays have been written by professional writers, unprofessional directors and private secretaries on the instructions of producers. Dialogues – usually considered an integral part of the screenplay – have often been written by a separate person, altogether disconnected from the person who wrote the screenplay for no reason other than that the writer of the screenplay wasn't familiar with Hindi! From these permutations and combinations have emerged interesting stories about life lessons, stray incidents, inspirations and the litres of perspiration that go into the making of a complete Hindi film script.

The script is not always complete before the shooting begins – and sometimes not even when it ends – but the journey is memorable nevertheless!

***Pyaasa*** (1957)

WRITING CREDITS *Dialogues:* Abrar Alvi

One evening during the making of *Mr and Mrs '55*, after shooting was wrapped up, Guru Dutt's long-term associate Abrar Alvi told him a story from his life.

When he was writing *Aar Paar* (1954), Alvi went out with a bunch of rich friends who had organized for a group of women to keep them company. Egged on by them, Alvi chose one of the girls and began talking to her. Her name was Gulabo. 'She had a sharp tongue and a sharper sense of humour,' he quotes in a biography, and it drew the author in him to her. Alvi never divulged any physical aspect of their relationship but mentioned that they had long conversations during which he found out about her birth into a decent family, her subsequent elopement with a lover who turned out to be married and her arrival at a brothel in Bombay. Gulabo soon became emotionally invested in the writer, for whom the involvement remained superficial. As he became busier with his film work, he began to renege on his weekly rendezvous with an increasingly upset – and ill – Gulabo. He felt intensely guilty – then and even later – but his priorities had changed. The relationship had carried on for three years, Alvi claimed, and ended in as dramatic a manner as it can get in Hindi cinema. While, returning from a film show, Alvi was on the top tier of a double-decker bus travelling along Grant Road, when he noticed a funeral procession going past. As his bus slowed down, from his seat, he could clearly see the face of the dead body on the bier. It was Gulabo.

At the time Alvi told Guru Dutt the story, Dutt was toying with a script idea about a rich gallery-owner's wife and her relationship with a poor artist. Dutt was so taken with Alvi's narration that in the story that got written the gallery-owner became a publisher, the artist became a poet (and the wife's former boyfriend) and the character of Gulabo became the muse. The on-screen Gulabo (Waheeda Rehman) was cast in the mould of the 'virginal prostitute' that Hindi film heroines usually are. She was much more refined and well-spoken than her real-life reference. But the prostitute did get immortalized through one of the classics of world cinema.

With Dutt's original idea and Alvi's final script coming together, the writing credits of *Pyaasa* remained rather cryptic. Alvi was credited for the dialogues but no one was credited for the story or the screenplay.

***Guide*** (1965)

WRITING CREDITS Based on R.K. Narayan's novel *The Guide*
*Screenplay and dialogue:* Vijay Anand

Dev Anand was in London when he read R.K. Narayan's acclaimed novel, *The Guide*, and wanted to create an international film in partnership with Nobel Prize-winner, Pearl S. Buck. The massive effort that followed led to a dud film in English but a classic one in Hindi – much to the delight of the actor–producer and the commensurate dismay of the book's author. The mild-mannered author was inducted into press conferences, location hunting trips, photo ops, script discussions and premiere shows – all of which, it seemed to him, had become more important than keeping the script faithful to his story. *Guide* is a classic example of how the Bombay film industry takes a novel, strips it of its local texture and adds on a kitschy pan-Indian layer to make it 'commercially viable'. The reason given to R.K. Narayan for shifting his story from Malgudi to Jaipur and Udaipur was that the widescreen, colour format of an international film necessitated a grand, spectacular location.

As for the story itself, the sparse narrative of a street-smart guide falling in love and eloping with a married woman were given layers of justification to make the concept of adultery palatable to a wide audience (and also to placate the moral police in the Ministry of Information and Broadcasting). In a trenchant piece about his experiences during the making of *Guide*, Narayan noted that the production team had actually bought out all available copies of the novel from Bombay's bookstores to distribute among those who were even remotely connected with the film. He observed that the director was constantly underlining text and making copious notes in the margins of a copy. Later, Narayan interpreted this as the director assiduously marking up the parts that were to be dropped from the film!

Probably the funniest part of the episode is the diametrically different ways in which Dev Anand and Narayan remembered the process. Dev Anand wrote in his autobiography about a phone call he made to R.K. Narayan from Los Angeles and described how the author was impressed and excited by his charisma. Narayan doesn't mention any such call in his piece and, in fact, indicates that it was a letter which preceded Dev Anand's visit to Mysore to secure the rights of the novel. He makes no mention of being impressed by the star at all (he says his nephews were). He was more concerned about the changes a film script may necessitate in his novel. As later events showed, his fears were not unfounded.

The end result (at least, the Hindi version) was not bad at all. In fact, it was an enjoyable and successful film. Except that there was no artistic reason to base the film on the novel. The producers wanted an internationally acclaimed Indian novel and an author whose 'presence was needed, not [his] voice'. The writing wasn't the key, the marketing was.

***Deewaar*** (1975)

WRITING CREDITS *Written by:* Salim-Javed

The traditional flow of script-writing for films starts with the producer (who may also be the director), his interest in a story/plot/idea/theme and a desire to cast a particular star. He then takes the germ of the script and a financial offer to the star, usually managing to bring him or her on board by tweaking one or the other. A writer is then employed to convert the idea into a complete script so that the inconvenient matter of filming can begin. This is how it has always happened. Except for a brief decade or so in the 100-year old history of Indian cinema, when it was done differently. When two writers cemented their reputation in the industry by turning this flow on its head.

Salim Khan and Javed Akhtar were almost like outlaws when they walked into the wild western town of Bombay. Being passionate supporters of an actor called Amitabh Bachchan, then a non-entity in the film world, they first went to him and narrated the script of *Deewaar*. Seeing his excitement and interest in the story, they 'chose' Yash Chopra as a potential director of the film and went to him with the script. (They had given Yash Chopra a three-line summary of the script which the director had liked.) In a way, then, both the lead player and the director were chosen by the writers – a situation unheard of in Hindi cinema. And it was not just Bachchan – they took the proposition to Shashi Kapoor as well, convincing him to take up the 'lesser' role, based on their conviction that it was strong enough to win him a Filmfare Award. As luck (and Salim–Javed) would have it, Shashi Kapoor won the only Filmfare Award of his career for *Deewaar* in the category of Best Supporting Actor.

The writing of the script itself was a dramatic affair. After their first narration to Yash Chopra, they wrote the script, with some of the dialogue, in a breathless burst of 18 days. In fact, they did this so fast that Yash Chopra's assistant director, Ramesh Talwar, refused to believe that they hadn't already had a written script when they'd made the initial offer! This is not so much the story of the writing or an inspiring story behind the film, as it is about writers being the prime movers in any commercial film industry anywhere in the world. Salim–Javed did what no one had done before and no one has done since.

## 49 BIOSCOPE

***Amar Akbar Anthony*** (1977)

WRITING CREDITS *Story idea:* Pushp Raj Sharma
*Story:* Mrs J.M. Desai
*Screenplay:* Prayag Raj
*Dialogue:* Kader Khan

In the mid-1970s, a Bombay newspaper reported the tragic story of a father who had deposited his three sons in a park and gone off to commit suicide. When film director Manmohan Desai read this news, he was more intrigued than saddened. That evening, his long-term collaborator, Prayag Raj, dropped by his home and Desai presented to him several interesting possibilities around the morning's story. What if the man didn't commit suicide but came back to find his sons missing? What could cause the sons to go missing? What if they were taken away by a Hindu, a Muslim and a Christian? Manmohan Desai, his wife and Prayag Raj jammed with this story till midnight. By this time, the writer had dropped his other plans and was ready to return the next day to work further on the story. Raj went on to write the screenplay for the film and the director's wife received a story credit for her ideas during that session!

For his previous film (*Roti*, 1974), Manmohan Desai had identified a part-time professor and theatre actor called Kader Khan to write the climax. Desai seemingly believed in a supremely illogical stereotype which he told Khan about when he was testing him: 'Muslim writers use very difficult Urdu words in their scripts!' But when Khan turned in his work, Manmohan Desai was delighted enough to raise his going fee (₹25,000) four-fold. Desai promptly signed him on for all his future films – four of which released in 1977 and were massive hits. *Amar Akbar Anthony* was among them.

Of the three characters whose story the film tells, Anthony was easily the most memorable and Manmohan Desai himself put forward valuable suggestions on the portrayal of that character, based on his own experiences. In the tightly packed Bombay neighbourhood of Khetwadi (where the director lived, literally from birth to death), Manmohan Desai knew a bootlegger who operated a hooch den just across his house. The cap at a jaunty angle, the leather jacket, the tapori lingo ('*Kya* Desai, *kaisaich? Dikhtaich nahin aajkal!*') – all of it came from Desai's neighbour. When his leading man expressed scepticism at what he termed as theatrics, Manmohan Desai grandly pronounced, 'After this film, people will not call you Amitabh. They will call you Anthony-bhai!' Like all his other pronouncements about the film, he was dead right about this one as well.

## 51 BIOSCOPE

***Jaane Bhi Do Yaaro*** (1983)

WRITING CREDITS *Story and screenplay:* Kundan Shah and Sudhir Mishra
*Dialogue:* Ranjit Kapoor, Satish Kaushik

Sometimes a script astounds you not only for what has gone into it but for what got left out of it.

*Jaane Bhi Do Yaaro* could be the top contender for scripts in this category. From the point where director Kundan Shah wrote a narrative (that vaguely resembled a screenplay) to the journey he undertook with his co-writers Ranjit Kapoor and Satish Kaushik to produce a shooting script to the final point where three-and-a-half hours of film had to be pared down to two hours and twenty-four minutes to meet the requirements of a lower tax slab – the journey of this script is mind-boggling, to say the least. Instead of going through the mechanics of the writing process, it would be fun to just list down ten things that didn't go into the final film:

1. A title song. When Vinod (Naseeruddin Shah's character) and Sudhir (Ravi Baswani's character) discover the editor of *Khabardar* is crooked, they sing 'Jaane bhi do yaaro, jo hota hai ho jaane do…'
2. A talking gorilla. In a cement warehouse, the duo encounter a gorilla which has escaped from

the zoo but is a sensitive, talkative character who pontificates on human inequality and suffering.

3. A semi-romantic relationship. This was to be between Sudhir and Tarneja's (Pankaj Kapoor's character) secretary-cum-moll that didn't go anywhere.
4. A game of chess. A game was to be played between Ahuja (Om Puri's character) and the dead body of Commissioner DeMello (played ably by Satish Shah), when the latter is brought home.
5. Poisoned puddings and photographic solutions in wine bottles… What more can be said about that?
6. A telephone conversation. To take place between a fake Ronald Reagan and a fake Margaret Thatcher.
7. A socialite called Palak Adamsee. It was written in as a dig at adman and theatre personality Alyque Padamsee.
8. A bathroom scene in which Tarneja's secretary takes dictation from her boss on toilet paper.
9. A somewhat muted climax in a video-game parlour and the rooftop of a skyscraper.
10. Disco Killer. This was slated to be Anupam Kher's role as an international contract killer brought

> in to kill the two photographers. Kher was much envied when this delicious comic role was given to him and pitied in equal measure when the track was dropped from the final edit.

Easily the darkest comedy in the history of Hindi cinema, *Jaane Bhi Do Yaaro* started as a script written by Kundan Shah called *Opening Ceremony* (which had many of the above gags). In a delightful coincidence, he registered that script with the Film Writers' Association on 1 April 1981.

***Jo Jeeta Wohi Sikandar*** (1992)

WRITING CREDITS *Story and screenplay:* Mansoor Khan
*Dialogue:* Nasir Hussain

We have often heard of kids who wanted to become a film-maker but had to join an engineering course because their family was full of engineers. Mansoor Khan was that kid in reverse! He studied Computer Science at IIT Mumbai, Cornell University and Massachusetts Institute of Technology. But he dropped out in the middle of it, returned to his family trade and directed *Qayamat Se Qayamat Tak* (*QSQT*) which was released in 1988 and is widely accepted as 'the film that revived Hindi cinema'.

In reality, the film he first started writing was *Jo Jeeta Wohi Sikandar* (*JJWS*), which eventually became his second venture. On his website, Mansoor Khan says, 'the theme of a boy who is a slacker and has to learn responsibility, closely mirrored my life.' Khan's restlessness led to his leaving some of the world's most prestigious institutes without completing his degree. This led to a feeling of guilt at not living up to his father's expectations, that he was a slacker, and it formed the core of the script – a boy trying to live up to his family's formidable reputation, without really being interested in their 'trade'.

The initial script he wrote did not have the father's character. It was about two brothers, one of whom was the father figure. Mansoor Khan later said the first script was in a 'whacko zone' and it was good that nothing came out of it. While he was struggling with this, his father Nasir Hussain asked him to direct a script that was already written – *Qayamat Se Qayamat Tak*. After its stupendous success, Khan had a clearer view of what would work in a film and rewrote *JJWS*. Taking the 'catharsis' of a wastrel as the central story, he made the cycle race – something he had seen in his own school, Bombay Scottish – as the final vehicle of redemption.

Mansoor Khan wrote what his cousin and lead actor of the film, Aamir Khan, called a 'very special script that could become a film for the times'. But, given his

Western sensibilities, Khan wasn't able to write the dialogues in Hindi and turned to his father, and writer par excellence, for assistance. Nasir Hussain translated his son's words into surprisingly youthful lines in Hindi (or Urdu, to be precise). He left only one line in English: Sanju (Aamir Khan) confronting Devika (Pooja Bedi) with 'But remember one thing, Devika, you're nothing but a bloody gold-digger!' One of the most memorable lines of the film.

(I can't resist adding here that the line had at least one negative fallout, when actress Nagma refused to play the role of Devika, which was first offered to her, because her mother was not happy with her daughter being called a 'gold-digger' even on screen!)

***Satya*** (1998)

WRITING CREDITS *Written by:* Saurabh Shukla and Anurag Kashyap

Manoj Bajpayee, who had acted in a small role in *Daud* (1997), introduced Anurag Kashyap to Ram Gopal Varma (popularly known as RGV), who was looking for a new writer. In his typical style, RGV told the 23-year-old Kashyap: 'Have you read Ayn Rand's *The Fountainhead*? Let's put Howard Roark in the Mumbai underworld.' By the time Kashyap – then an Ayn Rand fanatic – caught his breath, the director suggested an ending for the film that he remembered from a James

Hadley Chase novel. With no discussion of money or deadlines, RGV went off to New Zealand to shoot a song for *Daud*. When he returned, he asked for the script.

Kashyap was raring to go, but RGV decided to include a 'senior writer' who would write the dialogues and be a calming influence on the volatile Kashyap. This writer was Saurabh Shukla, who was suggested by Kashyap himself because the industry grapevine credited the older writer for ghost-writing the much-praised dialogues of *Is Raat Ki Subah Nahin* (1996). Saurabh Shukla suggested incorporating the domestic squabbles between Bhiku Mhatre and his wife into the script, giving the feared gangster a human dimension. The name of the central character, too, has an interesting story behind it. During one of the script discussions, RGV asked his office boy, 'Bhiku, *teen* coffee *lana*,' and the name stuck with Anurag. All these elements brought a distinct edge to the script that went on the floors in August 1997.

According to *Satya*'s editor Apoorva Asrani, the first day of the shoot changed everything. The scene they had planned to shoot was that of Sushant Singh's character trying to extort money from Satya and getting his cheek slashed instead. Anurag Kashyap later blogged that at the exact moment when Sushant Singh jerked backwards, so did RGV. The director claimed that he had finally understood what the film was about and that the script didn't work. (Quite late in the day, you would say!) To complicate matters, Gulshan Kumar was gunned down by the underworld and the script obviously could no longer say the things it had earlier wanted to.

Saurabh Shukla and Anurag Kashyap now rewrote the entire script – one that is considered today to be among the best screenplays of Hindi cinema.

***Rang De Basanti*** (2006)

WRITING CREDITS *Story and script:* Kamlesh Pandey
*Screenplay:* Rensil D'Silva and Rakeysh Omprakash Mehra
*Dialogue:* Rensil D'Silva, Prasoon Joshi

Kamlesh Pandey was an advertising copywriter. Rakeysh Mehra made advertising films. One evening, when they were shooting in Gujarat, they had a passionate discussion about the state of the country and the apathy of the youth. They decided to write a script that would introduce Indian revolutionaries, and their commitment and passion, from the 1919–1933 period to a whole new generation. After two years of research, Kamlesh Pandey finished writing the script for the rather cheesily named *The Young Guns of India*. But, around that time, Rakeysh Mehra got busy with the making of his first feature film (*Aks*, 2001) and the project was put on the backburner.

After *Aks* was completed, they wanted to start on the film right away but, putting their marketing brains to work, decided to test the storyline on youngsters in Delhi and Mumbai. To their disappointment, the story and the ideas were summarily rejected. They found that today's youth just couldn't connect with the youth from eight decades ago who chose to die for their motherland.

This is when they brought into the story an angle of relevance to present-day youth. As they discussed the broader issues, three threads emerged. One was the nature of Delhi University students, who are politically active in college but don't really act on their ideology once they graduate. The second was the occurrence of student movements like the protests at Tiananmen Square in 1989 in China and the anti-Mandal Commission agitation in India in 1990. Finally, there was a television news exposé on how substandard parts of aircraft were being procured for the MiG-21s, making them highly risky for use by the Air Force. Another advertising copywriter – Rensil D'Silva – joined them to sharpen the script and write the dialogues. He was much younger and was able to capture both the ethos and the language of the youth. Advertising guru Prasoon Joshi was roped in to write the dialogues in Hindi (because Rensil wrote in English) and he also wrote the lyrics for the songs, which fitted smoothly into the groove of the film. What started with *The Young Guns of India* thus ended up becoming *Rang De Basanti*, though the original name wasn't simply got rid of. In the film, the documentary that the character of Sue McKinley (Alice Patten) is shown making was given this title.

The writing and directing team of *Rang De Basanti* was entirely from the advertising industry. They used techniques they were familiar with – consumer research, for example – to gauge the impact of the script. Their expertise in creating widespread consumer acceptance through advertising stories also came in handy. The method of public protest – the demonstration at India Gate – shown in the film has since been adopted by millions of citizens to voice their demands and protest against injustice of any kind.

***Gangs of Wasseypur*** (2012)

WRITING CREDITS *Written by:* Anurag Kashyap, Zeishan Quadri, Akhilesh Jaiswal, Sachin K. Ladia

Zeishan Quadri had come to Mumbai to enter the film industry. While doing rounds of production offices, he watched several films with his roommates, Akhilesh and Sachin. One day, they saw the classic crime drama, *City of God* (2002). Zeishan wasn't impressed. If you think this is crime, you should see what happens in my hometown, Wasseypur, is what he effectively told his friends. Their initial disbelief was countered with a flurry of stories from Zeishan – one more unbelievable than the other – till they realized that in those stories there lay the possibility of a great script. They put together a treatment that they took to Anurag Kashyap (after a brief detour to Hansal Mehta).

The way they met Kashyap makes for a funny story. After reading in the papers that the director would be at Prithvi Theatre for a play starring Kalki Koechlin, then his partner, they went there and kept staring at the director till he asked them why they were staring at him! They made a hurried pitch in less than a minute, and it impressed Kashyap enough for him to ask them to bring him the treatment they had written. Although he liked the narration, he had the same credibility issues that Zeishan had initially faced from his friends. He asked the three writers to work on a detailed treatment and got busy with his next film, *The Girl in the Yellow Boots* (2011). When he got back to the youngsters after he had completed shooting the film, they had a treatment ready along with a pile of newspaper clippings. Those unbelievable events had happened after all! Kashyap immediately packed off a few assistants and two of the writers to Wasseypur to get more meat for the script. They returned after 40 days with more material than they had expected, much of it in the form of first-person accounts.

Nearly two years after his first brush with the story, Anurag Kashyap took the voluminous material from multiple treatments (including one written like a novel) and paper clippings and went to Madrid, where Kalki Koechlin was shooting for *Zindagi Na Milegi Dobara* (2011). In his hotel, he wrote the entire script for both parts of the film in about four or five days – getting it out of his system in one breathless burst. This is a case study of how realistic film-makers go about writing a script – with a fair bit of research and thought involved. Understanding that actors would be integral to the script and need time to prepare for their roles, they often also brief actors on characters during the writing process. The innumerable anecdotes about the making of the film would take up too much time and space. It will suffice to say the end-result was a cult classic that extended the boundaries not only of the structure of Hindi films but their language and look as well.

***Simran*** (2017)

WRITING CREDITS *Story, screenplay and dialogue:*
Apurva Asrani
*Additional story and dialogue:*
Kangana Ranaut

The traditional 'happy family' approach of screenwriting for Hindi films meant that everyone involved in the ideation and scripting got some sort of credit and, even if they didn't, they shrugged and moved on. The goodwill with a colleague counted for more. Many top screenwriters have 'polished' scripts for film-makers with whom they have friendly relationships without receiving credit or remuneration. When Salim Khan split from Javed Akhtar, he did this for several film-makers before he started writing solo scripts. He refuses to name his contributions even now, out of respect for the credited writers. Often, actors suggested additions to a character or improvisations to make the dialogues or a particular scene better, and neither do they take credit for what they add nor does a writer or director refuse their suggestions if the idea is good.

With Hansal Mehta's *Simran*, this kind of arrangement took a different turn amidst a flurry of allegations and counter-allegations. It started when the first teaser of the film was launched, giving writing credit to the lead actress Kangana Ranaut for 'Additional Story and Dialogue'. The original writer of the film, Apurva Asrani claimed that the film was based on his script and small suggestions made by the actress on set didn't merit a separate writing credit. This was in response to Kangana Ranaut's assertions that her inputs changed the film from a 'dark thriller about a drug addict' to a light, fun film with a broader appeal.

A comparison of the script (posted online by Asrani)

and the released film shows that Ranaut's claims are somewhat exaggerated. The script showed the boredom of the heroine's job as a hotel housekeeper building up, eventually pushing her over the edge. Without this nuance, her act of robbing banks to fund a gambling habit would have seemed abrupt. The script also showed the character researching the banks before she made her attempts to rob them, while the robberies in the film were depicted more as comic capers. While this possibly increased the popular appeal of the film, it ended up weakening the story. Also, the supporting cast of characters seems to have been reduced from the script, making the final film more of a Kangana Ranaut showcase than it was originally written to be.

Overall, while the changes seemed to be significant they did not radically alter the premise of the original script – something that has happened every now and then in film-making. However, the circus surrounding the issue was something else. SMSes, emails and conversations exchanged between the actress, writer and director were leaked. Multiple versions of the same event were bandied about. The three players changed sides – or people claimed they did – over a year-long period, in private and in public. *Simran* wasn't a pathbreaking film but it thrust the nuances of scriptwriting firmly into the limelight. There has always been gossip about how writers or directors change scripts to give one actor prominence over the other, but it had never been discussed openly or aggressively. *Simran* changed all that, for better or for worse.

## Ten stories, ten inspirations

***Afsar*** **(1950):** This Dev Anand–Suraiya starrer is based on a Nikolai Gogol play, *The Government Inspector*, in which a journalist is mistaken for a senior official by villagers.

***Bees Saal Baad*** **(1962):** Loosely based on Arthur Conan Doyle's *The Hounds of Baskerville*. Biswajeet's character returns to his native village in this film, only to become the target of attacks by a mysterious adversary. No Sherlock Holmes in this one, though.

***Kohraa*** **(1964):** A newly-wed bride comes to a lonely mansion only to realize all may not well with her husband and he may have had a previous wife – much like Daphne du Maurier's *Rebecca*!

***Gumnaam*** **(1965):** Agatha Christie's 'closed-island mystery' *And Then There Were None* received a desi twist and a cast that was the who's who of Hindi film character actors.

***Khudgarz*** **(1987):** Jeffrey Archer cribbed that Bollywood had ripped off his bestselling novel *Kane and Abel* to create the film about two sworn enemies. The film starred Jeetendra and Shatrughan Sinha in the lead roles.

***Maya Memsaab*** **(1993):** Ketan Mehta directed wife Deepa Sahi in the film version of Gustave Flaubert's *Madame Bovary*, the classic tale of a romance-obsessed, bored housewife.

***Saawariya*** **(2007):** Fyodor Dostoyevsky's *White Nights* was turned into Sanjay Leela Bhansali's stylized and flawed masterpiece, the film that launched Ranbir Kapoor and Sonam Kapoor in Bollywood.

***Aisha*** **(2010):** Jane Austen's *Emma* set in south Delhi, in which Sonam Kapoor went about matchmaking among her friends.

***Lootera*** **(2013):** The second half of Vikramaditya Motwane's charming period drama was taken from the classic O'Henry short story, *The Last Leaf*.

***Badlapur*** **(2015):** The plot of Sriram Raghavan's intense revenge saga of a man who has lost his wife and son seems to be inspired by the Italian novel *Death's Dark Abyss* by Massimo Carlotto.

# 4

# TERE GEET MERE BOL

## THE TEAMS BEHIND THE TUNES

A MEMORABLE DIALOGUE IN *LUCK BY CHANCE* (2009) states, 'Hollywood *mein* script *ko* property *kehte hain*', but in Bollywood (as the rejoinder goes), 'Property *ko hi* property *kehte hain.*' In other words, the script or story has very rarely been the draw in Hindi cinema. Mostly, it is the stars who are the draw. And after the stars, it is the music. The film-maker gets a music composer and lyricist on board, records a few kickass songs and, on the basis of this, starts scouting for financing. When Salim–Javed were writing the script of *Haathi Mere Saathi* (1971) on Rajesh Khanna's behest, the superstar got his favourite composers Laxmikant–Pyarelal to compose the title song. When the writers narrated the script to the producer, they played the song right at the juncture at which it would feature in the finished film – creating enough impact to get the producer to sign the cheque!

The importance of the composer and lyricist to a film is evident from the prominence they get on film posters – their names displayed more prominently than that of the writers of the film. While the choice of the two sets of people has mostly depended on the director and producer, sometimes composer–lyricist teams were so formidable that they became an unstoppable – and unforgettable – creative force.

## S.D. Burman and Sahir Ludhianvi

Sahir Ludhianvi, a leading Urdu poet of his time, had come to Bombay in the mid-1940s, but struggled hard to get work. His stature as a poet in the classical mould was, in fact, what inhibited producers from employing him as a lyricist because they weren't sure if he could churn out ditties that would be popular as film songs. Acting on a friend's tip, Ludhianvi literally walked into a hotel room where S.D. Burman was composing and was immediately asked to write lyrics for a tune the eccentric composer had created. At the time, Burman had no clue about Ludhianvi's stature as a poet and he was simply delighted that the young man could come up with excellent lyrics on the go!

Their partnership lasted a short time – about six years between the releases of their first and last films (1951–1957) – but it is easily one of the finest in the history of Hindi cinema. One of the first films in which they worked together was *Baazi* ('Tadbeer se bigdi hui taqdeer bana le'), which was followed by *Jaal* ('Yeh raat yeh chandni'), *Taxi Driver* ('Jaye toh jaye kahan'), *House No. 44* ('Teri duniya mein jeene se'), *Funtoosh* ('Dukhi man mere') and *Munimji* ('Jeevan ke safar mein rahi') – all of them featured blockbuster soundtracks. Dev Anand's career was made on the back of these films and their songs. When *Devdas* was remade (in 1955 with Dilip Kumar), they were the go-to duo who were instrumental in the new version being a clear break away from the legacy of the super-popular earlier version (made in 1936, with the legendary K.L. Saigal in the lead).

Having directed some of the earlier films they had worked on and knowing their musical depth, Guru Dutt turned to them for his magnum opus, *Pyaasa*. The music they created for that film turned out to be both their best work and their swansong. Never before had music, lyrics and the screenplay combined as perfectly as they did in *Pyaasa*. Ironically, it was this very film that led to their split. Ludhianvi firmly believed that it was the poetry that was the main draw and held primacy over the tune. He said this in a gathering where S.D. Burman was also present, and his views didn't go down well with the music director. Burman decided almost immediately that he would not work with Ludhianvi ever again. Thus, one of the greatest partnerships in the world of Hindi film music came to an abrupt and premature end.

### Naushad and Shakeel Badayuni

Very few composers have demonstrated the commitment Naushad had towards Shakeel Badayuni. The composer gave the lyricist his break in Hindi cinema (*Dard*, 1947) and, after that, he did not work with any other songwriter till the lyricists' death in 1970, except for just one film – *Saaz aur Awaaz* – for which he worked with Khumar Barabankvi, whom he had known before meeting Badayuni.

Theirs was not a partnership only known for the loyalty they displayed for each other. Naushad and Shakeel worked with film mogul Mehboob Khan in his massive hits like *Aan* ('Dil mein chhupake pyaar apna') and *Mother India* ('Duniya mein hum aaye hain'). Having worked with Dilip Kumar and impressed him, the duo became a regular feature in the star's films. It started with *Babul* (1950) and *Udan Khatola* (1955) but after *Kohinoor* ('Madhuban mein Radhika nache') they were the exclusive choice for Dilip Kumar's films with hit soundtracks like those for *Ganga Jumna* ('Naina lad jaihen'), *Leader* ('Mujhe duniya walon sharabi na samjhon'), *Dil Diya Dard Liya* ('Phir teri kahani yaad aayi'), *Aadmi* and *Sunghursh* ('Mere pass aao, nazar toh milao').

If poets like Majrooh Sultanpuri, Sahir Ludhianvi and Shailendra had clear political (read Leftist) leanings, Shakeel Badayuni was content writing love songs betraying no affiliation in his lyrics. This expertise and Naushad's classical repertoire merged perfectly in *Mughal-e-Azam* – easily their biggest musical hit. Apart from the iconic 'Pyar kiya toh darna kya', the songs 'Mohe panghat pe' and 'Mohabbat zindabad' were also huge hits. Although this may have been their greatest hit, it was not the only grand Mughalesque soundtrack they composed. *Baiju Bawra* (1952) – a film about the musician who challenged Tansen to a musical duel – was their other major success. It included hits like 'Tu Ganga ki mauj', 'O duniya ke rakhwale' and that beautiful symbol of secularism in Hindi cinema, 'Man tarpat Hari darshan ko aaj', the perfect bhajan composed by two Muslims.

### Shankar–Jaikishan and Shailendra

The glue that first firmly bonded one of Hindi cinema's most prolific musical partnerships was Raj Kapoor. The film-maker had spotted the poet Shailendra at a poetry recital and wanted him to write for his debut film. The Leftist poet initially didn't want to enter the commercial world of Hindi cinema but came around when he needed money for his child's delivery. The brilliant duo, Shankar–Jaikishan, was already composing for R.K. Films. Their partnership with Shailendra started with *Barsaat* and continued for nearly three decades, till the latter's death, and gave the world seventy-odd soundtracks of exceptional quality.

In this partnership, one must not forget a fourth member – Hasrat Jaipuri – who shared lyric-writing duties on many of the films. Shankar and Jaikishan often composed songs independently, though all the songs were released under their joint name. It is said that any one of the composers reached out to one of the two lyricists and went about composing a song. While Hasrat Jaipuri was also an exceptional poet, Shailendra was probably a cut above with his simple language always hitting home and his songs – while having strong social messages – never becoming slogans. Shankar–Jaikishan, on their part, remained committed to Shailendra, even passing up the opportunity to work with B.R. Chopra and Yash Chopra because they insisted on having Sahir Ludhianvi as the lyricist in their films.

For the R.K. Films banner alone, Shankar–Jaikishan and Shailendra created a roll-call of Hindi cinema's greatest soundtracks like those of *Awara* ('Awara hoon'), *Boot Polish* ('Nanhe munne bachche tere'), *Shree 420* ('Mera joota hain Japani' and 'Pyar hua ikrar hua'), *Jis Desh Mein Ganga Behti Hai* (the title song) and *Sangam* ('Bol Radha bol').

Raj Kapoor's acting career, too, was studded with exceptional songs written and composed by the trio. The films included *Chori Chori* ('Yeh raat bheegi bheegi'), *Kanhaiya* ('Ruk jaa o jaanewali'), *Anari* ('Kisi ki muskurahaton pe'), and most importantly Shailendra's own production, *Teesri Kasam*. Shailendra produced the film without compromising on the message he wanted to convey and ignored the popular elements that were known to contribute to a film's success. Despite critical acclaim (and winning the National Award for Best Film in 1967), *Teesri Kasam* flopped badly. Shankar–Jaikishan's excellent scores (songs like 'Duniya bananewale' and 'Paan khaye saiyan hamaro') for their partner couldn't save the film. Unable to take the pressures of film production and the massive financial losses, Shailendra passed away soon after.

Shailendra's final collaboration with Shankar–Jaikishan was for Raj Kapoor's magnum opus, *Mera Naam Joker*. While he passed away when the sets of the film were just being built, he wrote three songs for the film that were set to mesmerizing tunes and became massively popular when the film released nearly four years later. These included the first verse of what is called Raj Kapoor's – and later, the entire industry's – theme song, 'Jeena yahan, marna yahan, iske siwa jaana kahan'.

## R.D. Burman and Gulzar

'You and Gulzar do special things, don't you?' Asha Bhosle asks.

'Yes. I don't know how. Neither does Gulzar. But it happens. That's all,' R.D. Burman replies.

This innocuous conversation placed between songs in a 'best of' collection is an apt representation of probably the most magical musical combination of Hindi cinema.

Gulzar and R.D. Burman first met when Gulzar was writing lyrics for *Bandini* (1963), a film for which his father S.D. Burman was composing the music. They vibed well and their friendship grew to be quite strong. Naturally, when Gulzar began to work on his directorial venture *Parichay* (1972), he turned to R.D. Burman, known affectionately in the industry as Pancham. For the film, Gulzar had written the *mukhda* of 'Musafir hoon yaaron' and had given it to R.D., expecting a few days or weeks of creative consultation before the tune would be finalized. But that would have made the partnership normal. R.D. called him back later that night, at 1 a.m. to be precise, asking him to come over with his car. The two drove around the streets of Bombay that night, keeping the beat on the dashboard, and composed the tune that would be the first of many produced by this legendary collaboration. This was not the only time that a car featured in their creative journey. One instance stands out among others. As narrated by Gulzar in a memoir, Gulzar and R.D. had both stopped at a traffic signal one day. There was one car between them. The composer convinced the driver of that car to roll down his windows so that the Gulzar and he could jam right there on the street across cars!

From *Aandhi* ('Is mod se jaate hai') to *Kitaab* ('Dhanno ki aankhon mein raat ka surma') to *Ghar* ('Tere bina jiya jaye na') to *Namkeen* ('Panta bhatey tatka begun pora') to *Masoom* ('Lakdi ki kaathi') to *Ijaazat* ('Qatra qatra') – their collaborations have been a cornucopia of unique tunes, unusual wordplay and the unprecedented use of musical instruments. Their penchant for creating truly unique music was such that it became a running joke within R.D.'s music troupe. Whenever a really offbeat tune was composed, his troupe would say that no film-maker would accept it. Except for Gulzar. Their partnership was not about two professionals collaborating for a commercial venture, but rather two friends doing what they enjoyed most. Together, they changed Hindi film music in unexpected, unpredictable ways.

**Laxmikant–Pyarelal and Anand Bakshi**

During one of the thousands of music sittings this trio had during the course of their careers, Laxmikant was frustrated that they were not able to crack a song to fit a particular situation. He rose to leave and told his companions, 'Achha, toh hum chalte hain'. Almost as a reflex, Anand Bakshi asked 'Phir kab miloge?' – and the famous and popular song from *Aan Milo Sajna* (1970) was born.

When it came to Laxmikant–Pyarelal and Anand Bakshi it was all about their 'tuning'. Their long-standing collaboration started in the early 1960s and continued till the end of 1990s when Laxmikant passed away. At the time the duo was assisting Kalyanji–Anandji and Anand Bakshi was writing lyrics for them. They got along well and started off with *Mr X in Bombay* ('Mere mehboob qayamat hogi'). The partnership flourished and five of the Filmfare Awards that the duo won in their career (they won six in total) were for soundtracks written by Anand Bakshi. *Milan* (1967) had the famous song 'Saavan ka mahina, pawan kare shor' with the even more famous exclamation 'Arre baba, shor nahin sor… sor!' This addition was suggested by the music directors – in another example of their tuning.

With an uncanny knack for grasping song situations, and a penchant for using simple lyrics and catchy tunes, the three invariably rose to the occasion by producing chartbusting music for 'big films'. As a result, they became the favourites of all the 'showmen' in the industry. Raj Kapoor turned to them for *Bobby*, and they created the perfect soundtrack for it. They composed a procession of hits for Manmohan Desai's films like *Roti*, *Chacha Bhatija*, *Dharam Veer* (1977), *Amar Akbar Anthony*, *Naseeb* (1981) and *Coolie* (1983). But their most productive partnership with a film-maker that lasted for nearly two decades was with Subhash Ghai. Ghai's films were known for the quality of their music. *Karz* (1980), *Hero* (1983), *Ram Lakhan* (1989), *Saudagar* (1991) and *Khalnayak* (1993) built that reputation for him. For *Ram Lakhan*, Subhash Ghai had initially wanted R.D. Burman to create the music, but when Laxmikant–Pyarelal heard about the film they prevailed on him to give them a chance.

Be it the simplicity of *Ek Duuje Ke Liye* ('Hum bane tum bane') or the raucous fun of *Hum* ('Jumma chumma de de'), the traditional notes of *Sargam* ('Dafli wale dafli baja') or the youthful 'disco' feel of *Karz* ('Om shanti om'), the range of their lyrics and tunes is simply astounding.

**Bappi Lahiri and Indeevar**

In the 1980s, the Hindi film industry was in turmoil. Salim–Javed had split. Amitabh Bachchan had taken a break from films to try his hand at politics. The film-making giants of the past decades were ageing. It was in this era (which invested film fans sometimes call the 'worst decade' of Hindi cinema) that there was an onslaught of Hindi films by film-makers from

India's southern states. When you think of the films of this decade and much of the next, what comes to mind are Jeetendra in his white trousers, dance moves that resemble calisthenics, the introduction of casual vulgarity in dialogues and song lyrics, and insanely catchy music. It can safely be said that the last of these was entirely the doing of music composer and director Bappi Lahiri and Indeevar (as Shyamlal Babu Rai, a veteran lyricist, was known in the industry). Together, they created a riot of sound and words, so to speak.

A song in *Justice Chaudhury* (1983) had the line 'Mamma mia pom pom' and the use of 'pom pom' was justified (if that's what it can be called) by the presence of a jalopy in the picturization of the song. The entire song was, in fact, written in automobile terms: 'Pyar ki gaadi tez chalao, accelerator khub dabao'! The crazy use of unexpected metaphors was practically a trademark of the team that delivered massive hits like 'Ladki nahin hai tu lakdi ka khamba hai' (*Himmatwala*, 1983), 'Ek aankh maroon toh' (*Tohfa*, 1984) and 'Ooi amma ooi amma' (*Mawaali*, 1983). The last song was reprised in *The Dirty Picture* (2011) as 'Ooh la la ooh la la', a film set in Bollywood of the 1980s, indicating that its tune and lyrics were seen as defining elements in the 1980s genre of film music.

Fairly prolific through the 1980s and 1990s, the duo created music for other big-banner films like *Geraftaar*

('Dhoop mein nikla na karo') and gave Mithun Chakraborty a new lease of life after the 'disco phase' of his career, with films like *Waqt ki Awaz* (1988), *Guru* (1989) and *Prem Pratigya* (1989). In the mid-1990s, Hindi films began to be pilloried for containing vulgar lyrics, and Bappi Lahiri and Indeevar had something to do with that as well. They were responsible for a big chunk of the impossibly popular songs that contained lyrics replete with double entendres. One of the biggest hits of this time – *Aankhen* (1993), produced by David Dhawan – had the song 'O lal dupattewali' which is often cited as a copybook example of how Hindi cinema normalizes stalking. Another David Dhawan film, *Andaz* (1994), had the amazingly vulgar 'Khada hai, khada hai', which became a favourite in boys' hostels across the country.[2]

Bappi Lahiri and Indeevar's music has most often been dismissed as belonging to the hum-and-forget genre. Yet, one of the chartbusting hits of 2017, 'Tamma tamma' from *Badrinath Ki Dulhania*, was originally a Bappi Lahiri–Indeevar song from *Thanedaar* composed in 1990, and it's still rocking the discos three decades later. (Well, it was also lifted from a Mori Kante song, but I'm not going to get into that right now.)

---

[2] Both these films (and many similar ones) were produced by Pahlaj Nihalani, who brought in an era of *sanskar* and bhakti during his stint as the chairman of the Central Board of Film Certification (aka the censor board) from 2015 to 2017!

**Nadeem–Shravan and Sameer**

As mentioned above, Hindi film enthusiasts generally lament the declining quality of the music of films in the 1980s and talk about it hitting an absolute trough in the 1990s. This is not strictly accurate because several talented composers made their debuts during this decade and produced excellent music. Yet, none of them matched the impact that Nadeem–Shravan had, along with their favourite lyricist, Sameer. If awards are any indication of excellence, Nadeem–Shravan won a hat-trick of Filmfare Awards for Best Music in the early 1990s. All of their work from this time had lyrics written by Sameer. Even though Sameer has written lyrics for more film songs with Anand–Milind, his association with Nadeem–Shravan remains strongest in people's minds. The composer duo achieved this by agreeing on certain conditions with Sameer which included a promise that the lyricist would never work with Anu Malik, whom they considered to be their closest rival.

While all three of them were working on fringe projects since the 1980s, their hit-out-of-the-park moment arrived with *Aashiqui*, which featured a dozen songs that became superhits and made a clean sweep of the Filmfare Awards in the music-related categories in 1991. That year, *Aashiqui* won all four awards for music – best music direction, best lyricist, best playback singers, male (Kumar Sanu) and female (Anuradha

Paudwal). This had never happened before (at least, not since all four awards were instituted), and has happened only twice since - for *1942: A Love Story* in 1995 (R.D. Burman, Javed Akhtar, Kumar Sanu and Kavita Krishnamurthy) and *Lagaan* in 2002 (A.R. Rahman, Javed Akhtar, Udit Narayan and Alka Yagnik).

*Dil Hai ki Manta Nahin* (the title song), *Phool aur Kaante* ('Tumse milne ko dil karta hai'), *Sadak* ('Tumhein apna banane ki kasam'), *Saajan* ('Mera dil bhi kitna pagal hai'), *Deewana* ('Sochenge tumhe pyar') and *Raja Hindustani* ('Pardesi pardesi jaana nahin') were only some of the high points in their super-prolific partnership. (For those interested in trivia, Sameer features in the *Guinness Book of World Records* as the most prolific lyricist ever, having composed a staggering 3,524 songs as of December 2015. That's nearly three songs a week for 25 years straight!)

Their partnership hit the pause button when Nadeem was named as an accused in the murder of music baron Gulshan Kumar, and had to remain in London to avoid arrest. This was ironic because Nadeem–Shravan and Sameer - with their much-maligned *jhankaar* beats and simplistic lyrics - had become a rage and it was their success that had propelled Gulshan Kumar's company, T-Series, into becoming a musical powerhouse and a formidable force in the film industry. Say what you will about some of their songs being derivative or repetitive, as a trio they pretty much created one of the biggest production companies on the back of the records they sold. Quite an achievement, when you think about it.

### A.R. Rahman and Javed Akhtar

With the emergence of A.R. Rahman and his eventual rise to supremacy among music directors and composers in Hindi cinema, the epicentre of Hindi film music suddenly became Chennai, the maestro's home base. For many (if not most) of Rahman's compositions with Javed Akhtar, they never had formal sittings to discuss nuances or to 'jam' – quite unlike other composers and lyricists. Yet, their mutual understanding – based on respect and a sound knowledge of the nuances of music – never suffered. In an interview, Javed Akhtar recounted a story about the time when he had received the tune for the Ramleela song in *Swades* (2004). He was on a tight deadline because the recording had to happen the very next day to accommodate Rahman's travel plans for a music tour. He slept over it and wrote the lyrics for a fairly complex song ('Pal pal hai bhaari') that combined dialogues, music, traditional imagery from the Ramayan and a modern-day setting to present a completely fresh take on the Indian festival.

Rahman's partnership with Javed Akhtar started with Akhtar writing lyrics for original Tamil compositions that were being dubbed in Hindi. Matching both milieu and meter, he came up with songs for *Sapnay* (1997) and *Jeans* (1998) – both soundtracks becoming hits, even though the films did not. A film that is not often discussed but which defined their partnership came soon after: Deepa Mehta's *1947: Earth* (1998). Javed Akhtar's ability to capture the nuance of a bygone era through words and Rahman's ability to distil the era's essence through sound became something of a trademark of their combined genius. Their filmography shows a large number of period films they worked on for a variety of film-makers – *Zubeidaa* (2001), *Kisna: The Warrior Poet* (2005), *Netaji Subhas Chandra Bose: The Forgotten Hero* (2004), *Mangal Pandey: The Rising* (2005), *Jodhaa Akbar* (2008) and – most famously – *Lagaan*. Irrespective of the films' success, each of these soundtracks perfectly captured the mood of the time in which it was set. At a time when Hindi cinema was fixated on thumping beats and vulgar lyrics, the Rahman–Akhtar team bucked the trend steadfastly and was repeatedly rewarded for it.

Akhtar started his film career as part of a legendary duo, teaming up with Salim Khan to produce some of Hindi cinema's greatest screenplays. In the later part of his career, the Rahman–Akhtar duo turned out to be nearly as legendary, producing some of Hindi cinema's greatest soundtracks.

## Amit Trivedi and Amitabh Bhattacharya

In the early years of the 2000s, Amit Trivedi and Amitabh Bhattacharya were fellow strugglers in Bombay's film-music scene. Bhattacharya wanted to become a playback singer who wrote lyrics in his spare time. Trivedi was, meanwhile, composing ad jingles and working on non-film albums, when he met Bhattacharya while pitching to compose music for a television series and asked him to be the dummy singer for his tunes. Instead of writing dummy words to place in the tunes, Bhattacharya wrote the actual lyrics and Trivedi found that he really enjoyed them. The two hit it off brilliantly and another remarkable partnership was born.

When Amit Trivedi was offered his first film (*Dev. D*, 2009) by Anurag Kashyap, he reached out to Bhattacharya to write the lyrics. Nervous about his first film, he wanted a friend by his side! Since *Dev. D* subsequently got delayed, the two of them debuted with *Aamir*, an Anurag Kashyap production that released ahead of the bigger film. When *Dev. D* was released, what got noticed – apart from the jagged cinematography and psychedelic imagery that set the film apart – was what *Mint* called a 'brilliantly experimental score'. Their talent stood out clearly in songs like 'Emosanal attyachar', for which they took the standard trope of a wedding song and turned it into a cult hit to out-cult all cult hits! (It might interest trivia hunters to know that the song's lyrics started with 'Ek do teen chaar...chhe' – alluding to the missing *Paanch* in director Anurag Kashyap's life, the film he directed but never got to release!)

The success of *Dev. D* led to a slew of assignments that established the duo as a new-age composer–lyricist team who understood what the new generation was all about. Be it the slothful sexiness of 'Lazy lad' (*Ghanchakkar*, 2013) or the zany spoof of 'Dreamum Wakeuppam' (*Aiyyaa*, 2012), the soulful teenage hopefulness of 'Aazaadiyan' (*Udaan*, 2010) or the cynical energy of 'Dilli' (*No One Killed Jessica*, 2011), they always hit the right chords. Somewhere amidst the contemporaneity of their music, they also experimented with the 1960s jazz style in *Bombay Velvet* (released in 2015 and not very successful) and the dulcet retro style in *Lootera* (2013), arguably their best score till date. *Lootera* wasn't a great commercial success but songs like 'Shikayatein' and 'Manmarziyan' have ensured that just five years into their respective careers Amit Trivedi and Amitabh Bhattacharya have created an all-time classic Hindi film soundtrack.

### A Soloist for All Seasons, Majrooh Sultanpuri

If this chapter was intended to capture how music and lyrics have changed over the years – keeping the melody intact – then the last word has to be reserved for the man who didn't have a 'trademark team' but fitted in well with pretty much every composer – and he did this for over six decades.

Majrooh Sultanpuri was a Left-leaning poet. His radical political views led to him being jailed because he bitterly criticized Jawaharlal Nehru in one of his poems.[3] But that didn't stop the major composers and film-makers from continuing to work with him over the decades.

The admiration for his craft transcended generations – from S.D. Burman to R.D. Burman, from Chitragupt to Anand–Milind, and from Vijayeta Pandit to Jatin–Lalit. If there was a team of which he was part, it wasn't with a music director but with a film-maker. Ever since Nasir Hussain turned director, Sultanpuri was his only choice of lyricist. It was Sultanpuri who recommended R.D. Burman to Hussain for *Teesri Manzil* (1966)and created a trio of aces who continued to work together till the late 1970s. Even after Nasir Hussain retired from direction, Sultanpuri continued writing for his son Mansoor Khan and created evergreen hits, like 'Papa kehte hain' and 'Pehla nasha' for *Qayamat Se Qayamat Tak*. He was 78 years old when he was last nominated for the Filmfare Award for Best Lyricist

---

[3] A part of the poem goes: 'Aman ka jhanda iss dharti par, kisne kaha lehra na paye/ Yeh bhi koi Hitler ka hai chela, maar lo saathi jaane na paye / Commonwealth ka das hai Nehru, maar le saathi jaane na paye…' Such words about the prime minister of the country, for which he refused to apologize.

for the unabashedly youthful 'Aaj main upar, aasmaan neeche' in *Khamoshi: The Musical* (1996). He didn't win that award but by then he had been honoured with the prestigious Dadasaheb Phalke Award.

Easily one of the most popular lyricists of Hindi cinema, Majrooh Sultanpuri's talent as an Urdu poet has remained largely unknown. Very few people know that he wrote the well-known couplet: 'Main akela hi chala tha janib-e-manzil magar, log saath aate gaye aur caravan banta gaya'. We only remember the lyrics of his song from *Caravan* (1971), in which Monica-aa sang 'Piya tu ab toh aaja'.

## Ten songs that swept up awards

A selection of unforgettable songs whose composers and lyricists both won Filmfare Awards.

**'Jo wada kiya woh nibhana padega'** (*Taj Mahal*, 1963): Roshan and Sahir Ludhianvi

**'Chahoonga main tujhe shaam savere'** (*Dosti*, 1964): Laxmikant–Pyarelal and Majrooh Sultanpuri

**'Kabhie kabhie mere dil mein khayal aata hai'** (*Kabhi Kabhie*, 1976): Khayyam and Sahir Ludhianvi

**'Dil deewana bin sajna ke'** (*Maine Pyar Kiya*, 1989): Raamlaxman and Asad Bhopali

**'Ek ladki ko dekha toh aisa laga'** (*1942: A Love Story*, 1994): R.D. Burman and Javed Akhtar

**'Chhaiyan chhaiyan'** (*Dil Se*, 1998): A.R. Rahman and Gulzar

**'Ishq bina kya jeena yaaron'** (*Taal*, 1999): A.R. Rahman and Anand Bakshi

**'Kal ho naa ho'** (*Kal Ho Naa Ho*, 2003): Shankar–Ehsaan–Loy and Javed Akhtar

**'Nadaan parinde'** (*Rockstar*, 2011): A.R. Rahman and Irshad Kamil

**'Channa mereya'** (*Ae Dil Hai Mushkil*, 2016): Pritam and Amitabh Bhattacharya

# 5

# KHALNAYAK

## A BRIEF HISTORY OF BAD MEN

IN THE FILM *CHINA GATE*, WHEN THE FEARSOME bandit Jageera growls, 'Humse ladne ki himmat toh juta loge, par kameenapan kahan se laoge?' he may well be speaking for the entire pantheon of baddies in Hindi films. Indeed, villains in Hindi films come in many shades and degrees of evil. Yet, they don't merely provide a counterpoint to the heroic and the good. As screenwriter-lyricist Javed Akhtar once said, 'If you observe the villains of Hindi cinema over the last seventy years, you can write the socio-political history of India.' He was dead right! Hindi cinema has often been accused of influencing society in all the wrong ways. The truth is perhaps exactly the reverse. That is, just as Hindi films have been, for the most part, a reflection of Indian society, the villains of Hindi cinema too have changed with the times.

## The Troublesome Parent

In 1936, Sarat Chandra Chattopadhyay's classic novel *Devdas* was made into a film starring singer-actor K.L. Saigal. In 1955, it was remade – this time starring Dilip Kumar. Nearly five decades later, *Devdas* was made yet again with Shah Rukh Khan in the title role. All three films were huge hits of their time, going on to prove that if there is a really durable villain in Hindi cinema, it is the parent. While none of the versions of *Devdas* focus on the hero's father, it is the father who put paid to the craven lover boy's hopes of marrying his childhood sweetheart and turned him into a raging alcoholic. Thankfully, most heroes (and heroines) don't wilt under pressure like Devdas did. Look at who Prince Salim declared war against! The Emperor of India because the old fogey didn't want him to get involved with his dancing-girl sweetheart.

Be it Nazir Hussain standing at the top of a sweeping staircase, or Lalita Pawar standing in front of her dead husband's photo, her eye twitching with cruel intentions, or Amrish Puri standing in front of a departing train, the parent has usually been a symbol of oppression and rigid traditionalism – and thus, a formidable villain. Shammi Kapoor, christened the 'rebel star', rebelled (almost exclusively) in film after film against his rich parents in order to marry a girl from a less privileged background or against a rich girl's parents so she could marry a poor man such as himself. Shammi Kapoor's nephew Rishi and his grand-nephew Ranbir (not to mention, other romantic heroes down the ages) have all grappled with a fearsome father in their film careers – although changing times have brought along conflicts beyond their choice of a life-partner. With the turn of the century, villainy among parents has been often perceived differently. In *Wake Up Sid* (2009), which can well be called a villain-less film, the hero's father (played by Anupam Kher) tweaks the ears of the directionless hero and sets him off on the path to earning money. (Ugh, what an insensitive bastard!)

At the other end of the spectrum, heroines have had to rebel against their screen fathers, too, but the more prevalent struggle for them has been with their mothers-in-law! With arched eyebrows, venomous dialogues and iron hand in place, the mother-in-law has been haranguing heroines since time immemorial – most notably in films like *Sau Din Saas Ke* (1980) and *Beta* (1992).

**The Landed Extortionist**

In 1925, Mahatma Gandhi had said, 'India lives in her villages.'

This line caught the nation's imagination in such a tight grip that two decades after the words left the Mahatma's mouth, film-makers were still using it as a template to create characters on which to base their stories. In the beginning – say, within a decade following Independence – the setting of most films was a village and the hero was the poor villager. His adversary was the zamindar or the moneylender – a thorn in the flesh in real life as well. The centuries-old tradition of bonded labour and usury found creative expression in a number of classic as well as not-so-classic films.

In Bimal Roy's *Do Bigha Zamin* (1953), the cruel landowner (Murad) plotted to ensure that the small farmer left his village, tried to earn a living in an alien land and finally returned to see his dream disappear in a whiff of smoke. The creepy Sukhi Lala (Kanhaiyalal) of *Mother India* was in the familiar business of dispensing loans in return for usurping the land, wealth and lives of borrowers. This moneylender was not averse to using the borrower's compulsions (her hungry sons) to get her to sell her body. His evil nature became the direct counterpoint to the mother's sacrifices and her steady climb up to moral high-ground.

## The Dacoit

In *Mother India* the mother stood up to her son, who had turned to dacoity in the face of atrocities that he could not stop or protest against in any effective way from his station in life.

Whatever be the reason for his turning rogue, one

has to admit that there was inspiration enough around him as the ravines of the Chambal valley in central India were full of dreaded dacoits from the 1930s onwards, their activities and terror they unleashed intensifying in the 1940s and 1950s until the first high-profile bandit, Man Singh, was shot down by the police in 1955.

Interestingly, the portrayal of dacoits in Indian cinema has often been quite sympathetic. The real bandits of Chambal called themselves *baaghis* (rebels) against the system and this was probably true for many. Be it Sunil Dutt in *Mother India* or *Mujhe Jeene Do* (1963), or Dilip Kumar in *Ganga Jumna*, it was often the 'heroes' who played the dacoits and they always had a sympathetic back story. In *Jis Desh Mein Ganga Behti Hai* (1960), the central theme of the story was the balance of cruelty and humanity among the bandits.

On the initiative of social reformer Acharya Vinoba Bhave, an organized surrender (and rehabilitation) of dacoits was started in the 1960s, which continued into the 1970s, and the dacoits remained in the news and alive in people's imaginations through these decades too. In the 1970s, the filmi *daaku* started terrorizing people in his territory in films like *Mera Gaon Mera Desh* (1971), which starred Vinod Khanna as the villain Jabbar Singh, and most notably, *Sholay*. This was followed by a slew of lesser-known but aggressive enough dacoit–centric films. The last high-profile dacoit to surrender was Phoolan Devi, in 1983, and with that the glamour of banditry waned. The Sunny Deol–Meenakshi Seshadri starrer *Dacait* (1987) was one of the last big-budget dacoit films. After that, there have been some exceptions like *China Gate* (1998), but by this time bigger bandits had arrived on the scene and the moustachioed strongmen from the Chambal valley no longer featured as central characters in films.

## The Rich and Shady Businessman

While Nehru called dams, steel plants and institutes of science the 'temples of modern India', his countrymen (at least, those in the film world) didn't share his enthusiasm about any of this. In *Naya Daur*, the hero (Dilip Kumar) merrily drove a tonga and took up arms against a rich businessman (Jeevan) who started a bus service on the same route. Taking up the cause of 'Nehruvian socialism', the film ended happily with the tonga defeating the modern technology of the bus in a grossly unequal race.

The businessman as portrayed in Hindi cinema was almost always shady and plotting to increase his profits through a factory lockout here, some adulteration there and a bit of smuggling thrown in for good measure. The villains of Raj Kapoor's classics like *Awara* and *Shree 420* were industrialists while the hero was from the working class. As industrialization increased, so did the rich–poor divide, along with the sharpness of the portrayal of villains. At the beginning of the 1970s, we had the callous industrialist Vicky (Amitabh Bachchan) facing off against his working-class friend Somu (Rajesh Khanna) in *Namak Haraam*, while the 1970s ended with an unscrupulous mine-owner Dhanraj Puri (Prem Chopra) letting miners die for a few extra tonnes of coal as the working-class heroes rallied against him in *Kaala Patthar* (1979).

The working-class heroes – the *mazdoor*, the *kaamgaar*, the *mehnati insaan* – continued their protests and fights against the unscrupulous businessmen in the 1980s as Bombay reeled under the devastating strike of the textile mills.

### The Smuggler

The line between the businessman (say, one who adulterates food) and the smuggler (one who receives a load of gold on a deserted beach) is thin. You could say the former could become the latter with adequate practise. In fact, many of the smuggler-villains have adopted the façade of an honourable businessman to hoodwink the police. The legendary villain Ajit made his name as a suave antagonist in several films – most notably in *Zanjeer* (1973) and *Kalicharan* (1976) – in dapper suits, holding a cigar between his fingers and sporting a sneer.

In the days of the license raj and high import duties, even the rich had their grouses. Those who could afford gold couldn't buy it because of the Gold Control Act (1968) and smuggling became rampant. To counter this, the COFEPOSA (Conservation of Foreign Exchange and Prevention of Smuggling Activities) Act was passed in 1974 but, by then, the smuggler had become a defining villain in Hindi cinema.

However, smuggling was not the only negative thing happening around the country. As discontent grew, people literally took to the streets against corruption and misrule. The public mood was one of bitter cynicism and absolute mistrust of the government and a situation arose in which people were probably ready to be sympathetic even towards a smuggler. In fact, the greatest Hindi film to be made about smuggling was one in which the smuggler had every reason to be one. *Deewaar*'s Vijay Verma was a character born of the anger of the times – the decimation of workers' rights, the lack of rural employment forcing widespread migration, poor education and dismal urban infrastructure. So much so that the government could smell the anger in the air. As if on cue, around the time that *Deewaar* completed its silver jubilee, the Emergency was declared and the system appeared to have collapsed completely.

## The Ugly Politician

After the Emergency ended in 1977, India improved its stature as a democracy by booting out two successive governments for diametrically opposite reasons. The Congress party lost the 1977 elections for trying to gag the citizens of the country and suppress their fundamental rights through the Emergency, while the Janata Party-led coalition government that had come to power in 1977 lost in 1980 for not being able to work together at any level whatsoever. The two elections held in quick succession completely did away with Indian people's trust in figures of authority. In public imagination, which was soon to be reflected in every form of art, the politician became corrupt, the police officer dirty and the system untrustworthy.

Before the 1970s, the politician had a benign, peripheral presence in Hindi cinema. With the Emergency bringing politics to the centre stage, the evil politician was now very much the villain. It was a slow, gradual process, though. In *Mere Apne* (1971), a bunch of unemployed youngsters were used by politicians to fulfil their nefarious plans. In *Aandhi* (1975), the politician was more overtly nasty and indulged in dirty tricks to win elections. By the time Sadashiv Amrapurkar became famous with his portrayal of Rama Shetty in *Ardh Satya* (1983), the evil politician was firmly entrenched in depictions of contemporary society. As if that was not enough, the reigning superstar Amitabh Bachchan took them on in an electoral battle in *Coolie* and in a gunfight in *Inquilaab* (1984) and sealed the position of the neta as the premier villain of the 1980s. Even fading superstar Rajesh Khanna played the lead in *Aaj Ka MLA Ram Avtar*, a film that highlighted the farce that electoral politics in India had become. Defying expectations, it went on to become one of the biggest hits of 1984.

The troika of politician–industrialist–corrupt policeman still almost always appear together. Interestingly, in films like *Satya* (1998) and *Company* (2002), both set in the underworld, the main villain turns out to be the politician who controls both the criminals and the police, and with *Raajneeti* (2010) even the heroes started playing evil politicians!

## The Dons of the Underworld

With politics turning murky and the industrial scene really bleak, unemployment started forcing young people towards lives of crime. The Great Bombay textile mill strike went on for nearly a year after it started in 1982, and a large chunk of the original 2,50,000 workers never returned to work because the mills shut down. The underworld was around for quite some time in Bombay, as were the dons, but in the 1980s, their operations became more sinister. Drugs entered the fray and the stakes increased on both sides. As the notoriety of earlier dons like Haji Mastan and Karim Lala slowly receded, new gangs emerged led by the likes of Dawood Ibrahim and Chhota Rajan. The later lot were flashier, more openly confident of their deeds and given to ostentation. They, thus, became more amenable to filmi depictions. The earlier dons were 'anti-heroes' while the new dons were unabashed villains, a trend that really came into its own in the 1990s.

At the cusp of the 1980s and 1990s, there came gangster films like *Dayavan* (1988) and *Parinda* (1989), especially the latter, which attained cult status because of the legendary character Anna (played by Nana Patekar). One could posit that the massive success of Mani Ratnam's classic *Nayagan* (1987) – on which *Dayavan* was based – accelerated the adoption of underworld themes into Hindi films. The early 1990s saw the occasional films in this genre – *Agneepath* in 1990, starring Amitabh Bachchan, and *Aatish* in 1994 – but the villains were not the main draw of these films. The genre of 'don' films came into its own when Ram Gopal Varma almost single-handedly created it through films such as *Satya* and *Company* (2002). Of course, the moral ambiguity of the characters ensured that we were never sure if Satya, Bhiku Mhatre, Malik and Chandru were villains or heroes.

In the later part of the 1990s, the underworld had

become completely embroiled in the film industry – producing films, threatening rivals, promoting molls, even killing off producers – and this was also the period when gangster films were at their peak.

**The Foreign Hand**

When blonde-haired and gold-encrusted megalomaniac Mogambo strode around on a map of India in his high-tech den just off the Indian coast, he embodied the culmination of the trend of 'foreign villains' that had started in the late-1960s and continued well afterwards.

It is tempting for a chronicler of the history of Hindi cinema to link the emergence of this kind of villain to the rise of the 'foreign hand' in Indian political discourse. In October 1975, Prime Minister Indira Gandhi had claimed that 'foreign influences' were working in Indian institutes of higher learning to undermine her government. In the subsequent months and years, the spectre of the 'foreign hand' (always written within quotes) came back again and again – in the form of the Russian secret service (KGB), the American Central Investigation Agency (CIA) and other such shadowy organizations paying rogue Indian leaders and institutions to do their bidding. With the 'foreign hand' being held responsible for all of India's ills, the villains in Hindi cinema also got a foreign twist. International gangsters, spymasters and killers entered the fray, and from the looks of it they were here to create communal discord, supply arms to the Indian underworld and watch women belly-dancing in their lair.

While foreign villains popped up in films every now and then, the frequency of their appearance increased in the late 1970s. One could present *Parvarish* (1977) in which an erstwhile *daaku* (Amjad Khan) resurfaced with an accomplice, the foreign kingpin Supremo (Kader Khan). They had a snazzy den, an escape submarine and Tom Alter as a henchman. Around the same time came Ravikant Nagaich's spy series (*Surakshaa* in 1979, *Wardat* in 1981) starring Mithun Chakraborty as Gunmaster G9, which boasted of international criminals. While the ambitions of these film-makers were global, their budgets weren't. That barrier was broken by Ramesh Sippy for *Shaan* (1980), with the shiny-pated, shark-meister Shakaal (Kulbhushan Kharbanda) pulling strings in Mumbai from a nearby island. The post-*Sholay* Sippy coffers allowed for the villain to be presented in true James Bond-style, lavishly and creatively, making the international villain quite the thing in Hindi cinema. In a way, Shakaal was the precursor of Mogambo (*Mr India*, 1987) before the foreign villain degenerated into a caricature like, say, Dong in *Tahalka* (1992). In fact, the 'foreign hand' continued well into the 1990s but by then came to belong specifically to a particular nation.

## The Bothersome Neighbour

When Sunny Deol's character, Major Kuldeep Chandpuri, strode across the trenches in *Border* (1997), his booming voice alone could have caused the advancing tanks from Pakistan to disintegrate. Though one-off films like *Hindustan ki Kasam* (1973) had released earlier, it was *Border* that started a trend of films in which the villain was not a nameless foreign entity but Pakistan – our separated-at-birth sibling who had turned wayward. Indian films are almost always censored before they hit the video parlours of Pakistan but in the case of *Border*, the military police of the country made the parlour operators swear on the Quran that they wouldn't stock cassettes or VCDs of the film.

After the Kargil War (in 1999) and the success of *Border*, the floodgates opened, and Pakistan (especially their intelligence agency, the ISI) became a regular villain with some token good Pakistanis thrown as acknowledgement of old times.

The last two decades also saw a significant increase in realistic spy and action thrillers, requiring a readymade villain from across the border. Films like *Sarfarosh* (1999) outlined Pakistan's support for insurgency in India in meticulous detail. *Gadar: Ek Prem Katha* upped the ante even further with Sunny 'Scourge-e-Pakistan' Deol literally taking on the entire country of Pakistan in an effort to bring his wife and son back home to India.

Pakistan's rather blatant support of terrorism in India and the resultant escalation of animosity ensured the continued projection of Pakistani villainy. *Border* ended with a message about the futility of war and Pakistani soldiers were shown as equal victims of enmity, but by the time *The Ghazi Attack* (2017) was screened, even the soldiers had become snarling killing machines getting their just deserts. In fact, Pakistani villains became more frequently visible in all genres of Hindi cinema – and not just in ones depicting a war situation or in spy thrillers like *Baby* (2013) or *Agent Vinod* (2012), where their presence is understandable. Even a film like *Bhaag Milkha Bhaag* (2013), a bio-pic about the life of one of the world's greatest athletes, highlighted a relatively insignificant race in the athlete's career to show him slaying the demon of Partition.

**The Anti-hero**

While Hindi cinema has been faithful to the times and replicated the national zeitgeist in its villains, only a small group of actors typecast as villains have played these roles. Heroes have never ventured into this dark zone. When they have indulged in nasty stuff, it has been justified with elaborate back stories – murdered father, wronged mother, raped sister – and elevated their status to that of 'anti-heroes'.

This trend was broken by Shah Rukh Khan. In three films released five months apart (1993–1994), he upped his villainous deeds and negated the justifications for doing so, until his villainy became completely unjustified. In *Baazigar*, Ajay had a reason for murdering Seema (Shilpa Shetty) – revenge against her father. In *Darr*, Rahul stalked Kiran (Juhi Chawla) to the point of perversion without any reason but his mental instability (resulting from the hint about his mother's untimely death) was a sliver of a justification. In *Anjaam*, there was no reason whatsoever for Vijay ruining Shivani's (Madhuri Dixit) life and family. He was simply and purely a villain. (This part of Shah Rukh Khan's career showcases the meanest set of characters a Hindi film hero has played. Even the seemingly sweet Sunil of *Kabhi Haan Kabhi Naa* had an evil streak in him and went about creating rifts between his friends who were in love.) However, the audience found it difficult to accept the hero as the villain. 'Liberalization' had happened in economic terms but in cultural matters, India was not yet liberal enough. That would take another decade or so. Or not. Rajiv Rai's thriller *Gupt* (1997) created a sensation with Kajol cast as the main villain, although it could be argued that she had some justification – jilted love – for her extreme possessive and obsessive streak.

## The Coolest Ones

Sometime in the mid-2000s, it became cool to be a villain. John Abraham played a villain in *Dhoom* – where he was truly a rebel without a cause – which set the trend of getting major stars to play villains in the franchise with Hrithik Roshan and Aamir Khan following, thereafter.

Even yesteryears' stars got into the act and explored their dark sides…something their image didn't let them do in their prime. Amitabh Bachchan reportedly wanted to play Gabbar Singh when he had heard the script of the original *Sholay*. He got his wish in *Ram Gopal Varma Ki Aag* (2007) – but, as they say, 'Be careful what you wish for…' Rishi Kapoor had a dream run of badness when he played Dawood Ibrahim (*D-Day*, 2013), a child trafficker (*Agneepath*, 2012) and a corrupt cop (*Aurangzeb*, 2013) – all acclaimed performances and in complete contrast to the chocolate-boy hero the audience was familiar with. Sanjay Dutt threw his goofy good-guy image to the winds when he reprised the role of Kancha Cheena in the 2012 remake of *Agneepath*.

In recent years, with Hindi cinema becoming more experimental, audiences have been treated to more nuanced portrayals of villainy – a just-out-of-his-teens drug dealer (Tahir Raj Bhasin in *Mardaani*, 2014), an insurance agent (Saswata Chatterjee in *Kahaani*, 2012), a crazed police officer (Anurag Kashyap in *Akira*, 2014), an insensitive husband (Adil Hussain in *English Vinglish*, 2012) or even a bureaucratic coach (Girish Kulkarni in *Dangal*, 2017). They may not be the larger-than-life villains of yesteryears, but they display the baser nature of humanity in a more life-like fashion and situations than earlier. Oh, and one more thing: Did you notice that all the villains mentioned here were pitted against women protagonists in their respective films? The 'hero' in Hindi films is changing – and, clearly, so is the villain.

## Ten Devils' Workshops

***Sholay*:** Gabbar Singh's den was as stark as it was scary – with gigantic boulders, random pillars from a bygone era, and alcoves for cooking and living.

***Parvarish*:** A red wall with slinky dancers in silhouette, a pit with spiked walls to crush people to death, luxurious living quarters – a den reminiscent of a mega-villain in a James Bond film.

***Don*:** The 1976 film starring Amitabh Bachchan had many spaces for villainous cavorting – parlours, swimming pools, shady bedrooms and even a walk-in safe for storing loot.

***Shalimar*:** The den of this film's villain was a whole island, a massive palace, totally befitting an international master-thief.

***Shaan*:** An island with an underground den loaded with gadgets and gizmos and hungry crocodiles (not to mention hungry hounds) to eliminate enemies.

***Mr India*:** An island again, this time fitted with – hold your breath – a nuclear arsenal. It even had an acid vat in which the great Mogambo could melt friends and foes alike.

***Shiva*:** The local don Bhavani's den was a dark, dilapidated mansion with claustrophobic rooms and looked like it would swallow anyone who entered it and leave no trace of the person whatsoever.

***Agneepath*:** The stunner was not Kancha Cheena's swanky foreign pad but slum-lord Anna Shetty's citadel in a Mumbai slum. Surrounded for kilometres on all sides by homes of his loyalists, it was as secure as a den could ever get.

***Tahalka*:** A whole country. Yes, international criminal Dong ruled Dongrila, a country on India's northern borders, protected by snowy peaks, high walls and fiercely loyal guards.

***Fan*:** An anti-thesis to all the hi-fi villains' dens, psycho fan Gaurav Chandna's lair was a small room in a Delhi flat, plastered end-to-end with posters, photos and clippings of his hero.

# 6

# PARDESI, PARDESI

## THE EXPATS WE LOVE

HINDI CINEMA HAS SPREAD ITS LOVE TO THE STRANGEST of places. And received love from even stranger places. Raj Kapoor started a trend by becoming massively popular in Russia, a baton that was later picked up by – yes – Mithun Chakraborty! We have heard stories of Egyptian bandits letting Indians go because they are from the country that Amitabh Bachchan hails from. We have heard of traffic jams in Berlin caused by German women mobbing Shah Rukh Khan. In faraway Peru, flash mobs have danced to songs from Karan Johar's films. Aamir Khan's fan following in China has to be seen to be believed. (If we loosen the definition of Hindi cinema a little bit, then we have Japan going absolutely bonkers over Rajnikanth.) And for every star that has crossed over to a country, we have had someone or the other crossing over to India as well.

**Nadia**

One of the earliest *deewanis* of Hindi cinema was Mary Ann Evans. The name may sound like it belongs to an English novelist living in a quaint village in the United Kingdom, but Ms Evans was really one of the most exotic performers ever to have been part of Hindi cinema and she ruled the silver screen in the 1930s and 1940s. A fortune-teller once told her that success would come to her if she changed her name to one starting with 'N'. This led her to select the name Nadia for herself, and thanks to the roles she played in films she came to be called 'Fearless Nadia'.

Nadia had moved to India from Australia as a child, when her father's regiment moved here, just before the First World War. After her father's untimely death in the war, she moved to Peshawar, where she learnt riding, hunting and stunt moves like cartwheels and splits that would eventually make her famous. She honed her skills further as part of a dance and circus troupe. When she returned to Bombay, she moved between a couple of store assistant and stenographer jobs before she was recommended (by a cinema owner who saw her earlier performances) to Jamshed and Homi Wadia, whose production company Wadia Movietone specialized in producing mythological and 'stunt' films. Having heard about her stunts and impressed by her attitude, the Wadias launched her in – you guessed it – *Hunterwali*

(1935)! It was a Robin Hood-themed story with a distaff twist and the audiences lapped it up – as they did all the later films in which she starred. So popular were her films, in fact, that the eager crowds who gathered to watch them had to be routinely lathi-charged at the theatres.

Nadia spoke Hindi with a thick accent (that was almost comical) and was blonde with blue eyes. Some of her films used back stories to explain her 'foreign' looks, as if that mattered. She performed all the stunts herself – jumping from heights, lifting up burly men, running atop moving vehicles – often risking life and limb. Her devil-may-care attitude also led to a fair bit of skin show, the most famous instance being a near-nude bathing scene in *Hunterwali*. In film after film – *Diamond Queen* (1940), *Miss Frontier Mail* (1936), *Punjab Mail* (1939), and the delightfully alliterative *Hurricane Hansa* (1937) and *Lutaru Lalna* (1938) – she rocked the whip, horse and sword routine.

The years during which she was at her peak (1935–1943) were also the years that the Indian freedom struggle was raging. One wonders how, during this time, citizens of India oppressed under British rule were content to watch a distinctly foreign woman beat up their fellowmen by the dozen. A quasi-plausible explanation came from Mahesh Bhatt, whose father Nanabhai Bhatt directed Nadia in a film called *Muqabla*

(1942): 'Indian mythology has the attribute of feminine dominance. A woman can be gentle, compassionate and all-giving but she can also take up cudgels when need be. Nadia symbolized both these faces of the female mystique.'

This sounds as rational as any other explanation possibly could. What was not rational, however, was Nadia swinging off a chandelier and landing on her feet before disposing of some quivering goons with a swish of her whip. She was a star like no other and hers was a stardom that grew even after her time was over. It is said Kangana Ranaut's character in *Rangoon* (2017) was loosely based on Nadia as a tribute to her enduring charisma.

**Franz Osten**

Of all the foreigners who have made a mark in the Hindi film industry, Franz Osten is probably the least known. Yet, his partnership with Himanshu Rai – one of the pioneers of Hindi cinema – is as legendary as it can get.

Himanshu Rai, who co-founded the Bombay Talkies studio alongside his wife Devika Rani in 1934, had met Osten in Germany in 1924. Rai had come to Munich from London (where he was studying law) and the German producer was trying to make a series of films on religions of the world. One thing led to another and Osten and Rai's individual production companies got into a complicated arrangement that led to Osten directing a film called *The Light of Asia* and Rai playing the Buddha in it. The film was well-received in Europe and moderately well-received in India, but the response to it was enough for the duo to produce two more films – one on the Taj Mahal and the other on the dice game episode of the Mahabharata (with roles for Rai in both of them).

In 1934, Himanshu Rai returned to India and established the Bombay Talkies studio with the intention of producing films in India. To shore up technical expertise, he persuaded Osten to come to India along with a few other experts in cinematography and laboratory processing. (Among the cinematographers was Josef Wirsching, who came to Bombay with Osten and worked on several productions for Bombay Talkies. After Bombay Talkies folded up, he worked in some legendary films like *Mahal* [1949] and *Pakeezah* [1972], though he passed away in the middle of shooting the latter film.)

Osten's contribution to Bombay Talkies's success is undeniable. He directed the yet-to-be star Ashok Kumar in his debut *Jeevan Naiya* (1936) and in *Achhut Kanya* (1936), paving the way for the studio to thrive. He had his share of disagreements with Rai, but that did not affect his work in any way. For instance, he didn't much like Ashok Kumar from the time of his audition – neither the song he sang as part of his audition, nor his acting. In fact, Ashok Kumar's first few days of shooting were disastrous because the actor was too nervous to follow cues and instructions. Nevertheless, Osten manfully took on the misfit and got on with the job. Again, when V.H. Desai – a comedian with an unbelievably bad memory – flubbed his lines for the umpteenth time, he is reported to have said, 'Mr Desai, the problem is that the audience likes you. The moment you appear on the screen, it starts laughing. Had that not been the case, I would have lifted you myself and chucked you out today.' You could call it the famous German unemotional efficiency! Word has it that it was from his habit of calling Ashok Kumar 'Mr Kumar' (instead of Mr Ganguly, because his full name was Ashok Kumar Ganguly) that Himanshu Rai got the idea of using the anonymous, caste-agnostic 'Kumar' as a screen surname for the actor. This marked the beginning of a trend among actors in Hindi cinema of adopting pseudonyms with the suffix 'Kumar'.

Franz Osten directed nearly a dozen films in just four years, before the Second World War broke out in 1939 and he was arrested by the British because he was German. He was deported to Germany, where he lived until his in 1956.

**Helen**

You are not a Bollywood insider if you can't claim to have eaten Helen Aunty's khow suey. Helen may not be your aunty but she is the very famous stepmother of superstar Salman Khan. Helen Khan, nee Richardson, is legendary screenwriter Salim Khan's second wife and no less legendary herself. But why khow suey, you ask. Well, Helen was born in Rangoon to a Spanish-Burmese mother and a French father. When Helen's father passed away, her mother remarried, this time a British officer, and Helen took his surname, Richardson. The Japanese invasion of Burma forced the family to embark on an arduous trek to Dibrugarh in Assam from where they reached Calcutta and finally Bombay. Helen was about nine years old at the time.

To supplement her mother's income, Helen left school and trained in dancing. Thanks to her mother's contacts in the film industry, she got her first break in 1952 as a back-up dancer. After this, there was no looking back. After appearing in several films as a dancer, Helen's breakthrough came with *Howrah Bridge* (1958) with the superhit number 'Mera naam Chin Chin Choo'. Helen's performance in the song was the kind that audiences across the country still whistle at. It kicked off her career as a vamp (and frequently a cabaret-dancer), doing things no heroine would do.

In film after film – *Chinatown* (1962), *Gumnaam*

(1965), *Teesri Manzil*, *Jewel Thief* (1967), *Prince* (1969) and, most famously, *Caravan* – she was the dancer who took our breath away. Her slightly Oriental features, when supplemented with blonde wigs and foreign-sounding names (Suzie, Kitty Kelly, Monica-aa), turned her into an exotic seductress. While dance was her calling card, she also acted in small roles in quite a few films such as *Pagla Kahin Ka* (1970) and *Tum Haseen Main Jawaan* (1970).

After the end of a long-standing affair with producer P.N. Arora, her career hit a bit of a slowdown in the early 1970s, and it is at this point that she fell in love with Salim Khan. Khan recommended her for some meaty roles that expanded beyond dancing (though they hardly ever excluded dancing). Films like *Sholay*, *Immaan Dharam* (1977), *The Great Gambler* (1979), *Inkaar* (1978), *Dostana* (1980), *Don* (1978) gave her career a new lease of life till she settled down into happy domesticity and retired from films in the early 1980s. She has appeared on screen only occasionally after that, in roles that are typically tributes to her earlier body of work and which require her to shake a leg at least a bit.

In an interview, Helen had claimed that she has acted in a thousand films. Her biographer Jerry Pinto suggests that this is possibly an exaggeration and 'thousand' is really shorthand for 'many'. However, he estimates the number to be in the range of 700, which is still massive. This means that in a 25-year-long career, she acted in nearly thirty films per year. For cinema-goers in the 1960s and 1970s, there was a new Helen film in the theatres every other week. Even the most prolific character actors of Hindi cinema haven't done this amount of work. Considering the complexity of her dance moves, the costumes she wore and the sets constructed to be the backdrop for her performances, her commitment was of epic proportions and led to a highly deserved Lifetime Achievement Award at the Filmfare Awards in 1998.

**Bob Christo**

In July 1976, Parveen Babi was featured on the cover of *Time* magazine as the face of a story on Asia's 'frenetic film scene'. An Australian civil engineer called Robert John Christo was so smitten by her photograph that when he travelled to Bombay as a tourist, he wanted to meet the star. He befriended a cameraman whose unit was shooting on Juhu beach and used his contacts to meet Parveen Babi on the sets of *The Burning Train* (1980). He then befriended actor-producer Sanjay Khan, accompanied him to filmi party and there even took his side in a drunken brawl. A friendship developed between them, leading to a small role in Khan's production *Abdullah* (1980). This small role was noticed and soon more and more roles came his way. While *Abdullah* was the first film he shot for, some of the other films he simultaneously acted in released before it. His first film was thus *Arvind Desai ki Ajeeb Dastaan* (1978), where he played a carpet dealer named Mr Roberts. Soon, he became the premier wicked henchman of the villains through the 1980s and 1990s. His tall, strong, muscular physique made him an adversary fit to go up against the superstar heroes of the 1980s like Amitabh Bachchan and Mithun Chakraborty. And he never disappointed the audience as he put up a good fight before collapsing dramatically under the victorious might of the hero.

In his two active decades in Bollywood, the actor remembered as Bob Christo played pretty much every stereotype of the villainous foreigner. In *Kaalia* (1981), he was the intimidating jail inmate who said the iconic line that is usually attributed to Amitabh Bachchan, '*Hum jahan khade hote hain*, line *wahin se shuru hoti hai*.' In *Disco Dancer*, he was an international serial killer. In *Raaj Tilak* (1984), he was a gladiator. In *Mard* (1985), he was Simon (alluding to the man who headed of the eponymous Commission in British India). In *Jaadugar* (1989), he was the foreign follower of a shady guru. In *Agneepath*, he was the chief henchman of an international don. And, in what was probably his most famous role, in *Mr India* he was Mr Walcott, an 'exporter' of priceless antiquities who spoke the legendary line: 'Indian God maarta hai!' His Australian twang was used to good effect to taunt, harangue and threaten hapless Indian characters, whom he physically towered over. His heavily accented Hindi was probably the reason why the role of the main villains eluded him, as did comedians' roles. But even though he played a unidimensional character in film after film, often in blink-and-miss roles, Christo is easily one of the most recognizable character actors in India.

After two decades of starring as a Hindi film villain, Christo took on the job of a yoga instructor at Sanjay Khan's resort near Bangalore. When poor health forced him to retire, he took time off to pen his autobiography. He eventually died of a heart attack in 2011.

**Tom Alter**

Every other entry in this list is an expatriate in the true sense of the term. That is, he or she was born in another country and moved to India at some point in their lives. Tom Alter, though, is different. He may have been the most 'propah' sahib we saw on screen, but he was born in India (in Mussoorie, to be precise) to American parents. He was part of a generation of exceptional actors who joined the Film and Television Institute of India (FTII) in the early 1970s and graduated with their talents finely honed. One of Alter's earliest roles was in Satyajit Ray's first Hindi venture, *Shatranj ke Khilari* (1977), where he played Captain Weston, a British soldier familiar with Indian languages and customs. In a way, the role describes Alter almost perfectly.

Due to his looks, his role in a large number of films was that of the wily foreigner (with international names like Jackson, Rexson and Dunhill) out to conspire against India and Indians. While Bob Christo's burly frame made him the ideal candidate for a brawny henchman, Tom Alter was cast most aptly as the smooth-talking nasty. Films like *Parvarish*, *Kranti* (1981), *Karma* (1986), *Tridev* (1989) and *Tahalka* had him playing the foreign devil but he was versatile enough to play Indian characters too. His portrayal of the sophisticated don Musa in *Parinda* is a case in point, where he was a worthy adversary to the star-studded gang of Nana Patekar, Jackie Shroff and Anil Kapoor. It is a testament to his adaptability that he has played both Lord Mountbatten (*Sardar*, 1993) and Maulana Abul Kalam Azad (in the television series *Samvidhaan*, 2014) on screen.

Beyond cinema, he briefly worked as a sports journalist in the late 1980s, during the course of which he is credited to have conducted the first ever video interview of Sachin Tendulkar in 1989. For his work in cinema, theatre, television and literature (he wrote three books), Tom Alter was awarded the Padma Shri in 2008. Quite tragically, he succumbed to bone cancer in 2017 at the age of 67.

**Nusrat Fateh Ali Khan**

When teen heart-throbs Rishi Kapoor and Neetu Singh decided to get married in January 1980, the entire film industry was abuzz. The groom's father was the resident showman of the industry and he didn't disappoint. For the sangeet, Raj Kapoor flew in a Pakistani *qawwali* singer and his troupe. The singer was Ustad Nusrat Fateh Ali Khan.

Part of a 600-year-old *gharana*, Nusrat sahab was born to sing. And sing he did. From his early teens, he sang as part of his father's troupe and continued to do so even after his father's death. His rise as an out-of-the-world *qawwali* singer was bolstered by his brilliant compositions and his performances in the USA and Europe. He composed, or was deeply involved in the development of, high-profile Hollywood soundtracks like *The Last Temptation of Christ* (1988), *Natural Born Killers* (1994) and *Dead Man Walking* (1995). While he was composing these or performing at the Royal Albert Hall in London, he was known in India only among music aficionados. Nusrat sahab broke into Indian consciousness with a series of music videos in the early 1990s when MTV started broadcasting in India. His classic *qawwali*s – 'Jhoole jhoole lal' and 'Kinna sona tenu' – were first broadcast in the country as remixes and ruled the airwaves, taking the film industry by storm. Soon afterwards, in 1996, he sang 'Afreen afreen' (picturized on Lisa Ray in a memorable video) and it instantly made him a sensation among music-lovers and Bollywood producers alike.

Nusrat sahab composed the music for just four films (*Bandit Queen* [1994], *Aur Pyaar Ho Gaya* [1997], *Kartoos* [1999] and *Kachche Dhaage* [1999]) and sang for or featured just in a handful more. His voice and music had a special quality that transcended all boundaries and mesmerized listeners. His career in India was extremely short (he passed away in 1997) but his impact has lingered – unfortunately, through the astounding number of rip-offs of his songs in Hindi films. Being the gentle soul that he was, Nusrat sahab made peace with the plagiarism, but was reported to have been particularly aggrieved when Anu Malik turned his spiritual 'Allah hoo Allah hoo' into 'I love you, I love you'!

His legend lives on. His haunting voice and music imbued with spirituality embody the true spirit of the *qawwali*, which is increasingly becoming a lost art. Nearly two decades after his demise, he is still the gold standard of what he himself called 'roohani' (divine) music.

**Manisha Koirala**

Readers may experience a moment of incomprehension when they find Manisha Koirala being referred to as an expat. Though she studied in Varanasi and Delhi, Koirala is the granddaughter of Bishweshwar Prasad Koirala, the former prime minister of Nepal. During a break after her board exams, she acted in a Nepali film as a lark and liked the experience enough to move to Bombay to try her luck in Hindi films.

The move worked out exceptionally well for her as several top-notch film-makers made her offers almost on the spot. Shekhar Kapur signed her on for *Dushmani*, but the film never got made. Boney Kapoor, then trying to launch his youngest brother Sanjay, offered her a role in *Prem* (1995) if Tabu (who was already selected and was having second thoughts) didn't come through. Rishi Kapoor offered her the role of the second lead in *Henna* (1991), which the supremely confident newcomer refused! Finally, the film she debuted in was Subhash Ghai's blockbuster *Saudagar* (1991), where she played the romantic lead and held her own in the acting department, grabbing attention amidst the battle of the thespians between Dilip Kumar and Raaj Kumar. Despite some indifferent performances that followed, Manisha Koirala's hallmark remains her ability to turn in powerhouse performances for big directors. Her performances with directors like Mani Ratnam

(*Bombay*, 1995 and *Dil Se..*, 1998), Vidhu Vinod Chopra (*1942: A Love Story*), Sanjay Leela Bhansali (*Khamoshi: The Musical*) and Rajkumar Santoshi (*Lajja*, 2001), rank among the best of her times. Even in a derivative film like *Agni Sakshi* (1996), her performance as a tortured wife was pitch-perfect against the formidable Nana Patekar.

As with many other female actors in Hindi films, she drifted away from films and got married, which ended in divorce. She was diagnosed with ovarian cancer in 2012 but her treatment has been successful and she is now cancer-free. At the time of this book going to press, she is scheduled to play the role of Nargis in Sanjay Dutt's biopic, directed by Rajkumar Hirani. This could possibly be the role that brings her back into the limelight.

**Katrina Kaif**

Although nobody could have predicted it from the performance of her debut film, Katrina Kaif is perhaps the most successful expatriate actor in Hindi cinema by a very long mile.

Born to British parents (though her father is of Kashmiri descent) in Hong Kong, she was raised in London and took her mother's surname when her parents divorced. She remained Katrina Turquotte until changing her surname to 'Kaif', as recommended to her when she signed her first film in 2003. Ayesha

Shroff, the producer of the film, also mentioned in an interview that 'We wanted to give her a surname which would be accepted by the Indian audience... So we thought of Kaif.' Katrina, however, denied this and stuck to her version of the story – that her estranged father, a Kashmiri, lives in the USA.

The film that these stories were supposedly created for ranks among the worst commercial and critical disasters in the history of Hindi cinema – *Boom*. Katrina was primarily selected for it because she had a really fit body and was not averse to wearing a bikini in then-conservative Bollywood. She performed as well as she could in that nuclear wasteland of a film, and remains the only one among the three heroines of the film to have made a career in acting. But even that required a cooling-off period during which she acted in a couple of Telugu films (*Malliswari*, 2004 and *Allari Pidugu*, 2005) and one in Malayalam (*Balram vs. Tharadas*, 2006).

She restarted her career in Hindi cinema with short roles (*Sarkar*, 2005), low-key roles (*Maine Pyaar Kyun Kiya*, 2005) and medium-key roles (*Partner*, 2007) before hitting it big-time with *Namastey London* (2007) and *Welcome* (2007). After this, she has acted in some of the biggest hits of recent times – partnering with Akshay Kumar in *Singh is Kinng* (2008) and Salman Khan in *Ek Tha Tiger* (2012) and *Tiger Zinda Hai* (2017), among others. Though her acting and her heavily accented

Hindi have come up for severe criticism, every director she has worked with vouches for her professionalism and hardworking nature. Cleverly casting her as an NRI or expatriate, directors have managed to build her diction into the script. To be fair, she has by now got noticed in what the industry calls 'performance-oriented roles', in *Raajneeti* and *Zindagi Na Milegi Dobara.*

Apart from commercial success, Katrina Kaif has remained in the news for her much-publicized affairs (first with Salman Khan and then with Ranbir Kapoor), her superbly promoted item numbers ('Chikni Chameli' and 'Sheila ki jawaani'), and in the film *Bombay Talkies*, in which she didn't really appear, she was shown as the epitome of female stardom that children aspire to. That she has, and is, working alongside the fastidious Aamir Khan (in *Dhoom 3* and the forthcoming *Thugs of Hindostan*) says quite a bit about her ability to deliver. Indeed, as discussions about nepotism in the industry rage on, a British woman with no industry connections making it to the top is quite an achievement.

**Fawad Khan**

Pakistan has exported several stars to India over the last few decades, starting mainly from the 1980s. After the tensions of Partition and the subsequent wars subsided, a steady stream of Pakistani actors of varying ability have entered the Hindi film industry. Indian audiences have never been too discerning about the origins of actors, an observation best borne out by the fact that Pakistani cricketer Mohsin Khan secured lead roles in a few films when his only qualification was his marriage to the actress Reena Roy. Somy Ali, too, joined the industry in the 1990s, but her claim to fame became her relationship with Salman Khan rather than her performances. By and large, Pakistan's exports to India have been in the music department and actors have been relatively few. Ali Zafar, also of Pakistani descent, is essentially a singer who branched into acting. This changed somewhat with the phenomenon called Fawad Khan, the first Pakistani to feature on the cover of *Filmfare* magazine.

Fawad Khan's father was born in Patiala and moved to Pakistan during the Partition. His film debut in Pakistan was in *Khuda Kay Liye* (the Indian connection to the film was Naseeruddin Shah who played a cameo in it). After its release, Fawad Khan became a bit of a sensation in Pakistan with a slew of popular films and television shows to his credit. The tipping point in India came when Zee Entertainment Enterprises Ltd launched a new television channel called Zindagi that aired international shows dubbed in Hindi. Among the shows on the channel was Fawad Khan-starrer *Zindagi Gulzar Hai*, which became an instant hit among viewers, mainly women. Soon his other shows, telefilms and even trailers were being viewed by thousands on YouTube. Presumably this is what prompted the casting director of *Khoobsurat* – a remake of the Hrishikesh Mukherjee-directed film of the 1980s – to approach Fawad Khan for a lead role opposite Sonam Kapoor.

*Khoobsurat* got a lukewarm response at the box office but Fawad was noticed and fawned over, and was awarded the Filmfare Award for Best Male Debut in 2015. From here on, he hit it big when he was signed on to play a pivotal role in the Karan Johar production *Kapoor & Sons (Since 1921)* (2016). In a film packed with solid actors, he delivered probably the most noticeable performance and looked set for a major career in Hindi cinema. Then came *Ae Dil Hai Mushkil* (2016), also a Karan Johar film, and audiences waited in anticipation to watch another spectacular performance from Fawad Khan. But this was not to be. The release of the film coincided with several terror attacks on Indian Army camps by Pakistan and nationalist groups within India launched vociferous protests against Pakistani actors being cast in Indian films. Fawad Khan's role in *Ae Dil Hai Mushkil* was allegedly chopped down, his character (a Pakistani in the original script) was made an Indian and he was kept out of all promotions of the film. He eventually returned to Pakistan, leaving behind broken hearts among women and liberal secularists alike.

It is interesting to note that with just three Hindi

films, Fawad Khan has become a bigger craze in India than many Pakistani actors and singers who have had much longer stints. Thanks to video streaming, social-media fan clubs and discussion boards, he has been the star who made Indian women fans swoon and scream. That he has displayed great acting skills almost seems like a bonus. In the 1990s, the standard Indo-Pakistani banter was that if India would give up Madhuri Dixit, Pakistan would give up all claims to Kashmir. With Fawad Khan, the two countries have probably got a viable trading option.

**Sunny Leone**

Raj Nayak, head honcho of the television channel Colors, was told during a content meeting for the super-popular show *Bigg Boss* that the team had paid a fee to an Indo-Canadian star to appear on the show, but was not sure if they should have. On learning about the nature of the films she produced and acted in, Nayak asked if she would do anything similar on Indian television. On being assured that she would not, he told his team to get the girl on the show since her fees had been paid anyway. He forgot all about it till his team reminded him on the day the star landed in India. Wanting to find out more about the star, he looked her up on Google and sat open-mouthed when the images and videos popped up. Well, the star in question, Sunny Leone does have that effect on people!

Born in Canada, Karenjit Kaur Vohra moved to the USA and was dreading a career as a receptionist when she got an opportunity to work in what is euphemistically called the 'adult entertainment industry'. She wasn't sure what it entailed, but when she heard about the money she would be paid, her first thought was, 'How hard can it be?', and signed up. Her career took off and she was soon featured in magazines such as *Penthouse* and *Hustler*. Vivid Entertainment – otherwise known as the Warner Bros. of adult films – took her on as a star and she became wildly popular. In 2009, she branched out into production by launching her own company – SunLust Pictures – with her then partner (and now husband) Daniel Weber and was contemplating her next move when the call from Colors came along. And the rest was Raj Nayak's search history!

In India, her popularity exploded when Mahesh Bhatt landed up in the *Bigg Boss* house to offer her a role in *Jism 2*. (Pooja Bhatt has claimed that she had spotted Sunny way back in 2002 when she was casting for *Jism*. On learning that she was with *Penthouse*, Bhatt backed off but remembered her till a decade later when she came on *Bigg Boss*.) Leone has not looked back since. Most of her film roles have been as an 'item girl' but she has managed to get lead roles as well (*Jackpot* [2013], *Ek Paheli Leela* [2015] and *One Night Stand* [2016]).

Apart from her films, her disarming charm during public appearances and her straight-talking, candid interviews have won her admiration from large groups of people. When a television anchor was condescending towards her during an interview, she received an avalanche of support on both social and mainstream media. When she appears in public places, the crowds that throng to see her equal – and often exceed – those attracted by top stars and political leaders.

The biggest impact that Sunny Leone has had as an expatriate performer is the dignity with which she conducts her life – with regards to both her past and the present. Her porn-star past is seen by large sections of people as something a working girl did with diligence and passion. Her accent and basic acting prowess seem irrelevant after that. It is probably a sign of the times that Indians – women included – view her with the affection they reserve for their favourite stars. This is evident if one studies Google search trends. For four years in a row since she arrived in India[4] (2012–2015), Sunny Leone has been the most searched person on Google. Yes, that means she even beat Narendra Modi in 2014.

---

[4] Strictly speaking, she appeared on MTV India as a red carpet reporter at the MTV Video Music Awards (but obviously the show wasn't Indian).

## Ten Indian actors abroad

**I.S. Johar**, the funny man of Hindi cinema, performed in cameo roles in Hollywood films like *Lawrence of Arabia* and *Death on the Nile*.

**Kabir Bedi** played an Indian pirate in an Italian television series, *Sandokan*, which brought him unexpected stardom in Italy. Also seen in a Bond film, *Octopussy*.

**Persis Khambatta**, the winner of the Miss India crown in 1965, shaved her head to play Lieutenant Ilia in *Star Trek: The Movie*.

**Amrish Puri** acquired Steven Spielberg as a fan after his super-villain act in *Indiana Jones and the Temple of Doom*.

**Om Puri** had a short but powerful role in Richard Attenborough's *Gandhi*, and went on to act in several Hollywood and British productions like *Wolf* (with Jack Nicholson), *The Ghost and the Darkness* (with Michael Douglas and Val Kilmer) and *East is East*.

**Irrfan** has starred in a number of international films, from art-house classics (*The Namesake* with Tabu) to superhero blockbusters (*The Amazing Spiderman*).

**Naseeruddin Shah** claimed to have recovered the costs of many years of acting in theatre productions with his Captain Nemo act in *The League of Extraordinary Gentlemen*.

**Amitabh Bachchan** garnered extremely positive reviews in a blink-and-you-miss-it role as a Jewish gambler, Meyer Wolfsheim, in the Leonard DiCaprio starrer *The Great Gatsby*.

**Deepika Padukone** played a substantial role opposite Vin Diesel in *xXx: Return of Xander Cage*, complete with guns, grenades and sexy costumes.

**Priyanka Chopra** has been noticed all over Hollywood from 2015 onwards – in television shows (*Quantico*, which top lined her), films (*Baywatch*) and at awards nights as a presenter at the Oscar Awards in 2016 – and looks good for more!

# 7

# SAATH SAATH, ALAG ALAG

## DIFFERENT THINGS SAID, THINGS SUNG DIFFERENTLY

AN OFT-REPEATED COMPLAINT AGAINST HINDI FILMS IS the set, predictable pattern of the way the plot unfolds in film after film.

Boy meets girl. Boy loses girl. Boy gets girl. In between they sing.

Boy loves country. Boy fights for country. Boy gets girl. In between they sing.

Boy has a brother. Boy loses brother. Boy reunites with brother. Boy gets girl. In between they sing.

It's evident then that whatever twist a plot may have, there is always a suitable song to heighten the emotion, give insight into a character or simply allow the audience to escape into the world created by the film. Although with changing times new situations and settings are beginning to introduce some variation in the usual plot, today's protagonists largely continue to experience situations similar to their predecessors. Yet, their response to the same situations has changed somewhat. And what can be a better indication of such change than the songs they sing and the lyrics that convey the drama of any given moment.

**Songs of Love**

Since love songs in films appear at opportune moments in the story, they can be classified into different stages of romance.

There were the songs inviting love that were sung when the lead player was in the process of wooing the person of interest. (I say 'lead player' because in Hindi films women hardly shy away from wooing their men.) Invariably, the woo-er tunefully promised the object of affection the moon and stars and other celestial forms of happiness. In *Kismat* (1968), for instance, the lady, albeit in a slightly drunken state, crooned, 'Aao huzoor, tumko sitaron mein le chaloon,' suggesting much more than the words expressed. Many years later, in *Ghulam* (1998), a Mumbai *tapori*, Siddhu, expressed a similar intention using a very different expression, when he asked a posh girl from south Bombay to come with him on a trip with the spunky offer 'Aati kya Khandala?'. According to purists, this proposal, made boldly and casually, ended the era of poetry in Hindi films. Gone were the promises of ethereal bliss. Here was the earthier option of togetherness – eating chikkis and taking photographs after visiting the local sights. But who is anyone to comment on the lack of poetic expression if the lady in question is suitably impressed by the proposition and the purpose has been served?

As the love story progressed, the man often saw in his beloved manifestations of the most beautiful things in the universe. In *Chaudhvin ka Chand*, Guru Dutt, playing the pensive, love-struck Aslam, sang 'Chaudhvin ka chand ho, ya aftab ho, jo bhi ho tum khuda ki kasam lajawab ho'. Enamoured by the ethereal beauty of Jameela (Waheeda Rehman), he saw in her the beauty of the moon and the brightness of the sun. The tradition continued well into the 1990s. In *1942: A Love Story*, Narendra Singh (Anil Kapoor) compared his beloved Rajeshwari (Manisha Koirala) to a multitude of beautiful things – all of them adding to her effect on him like small brushstrokes in an exquisite painting: she was a budding rose, a poet's dream, the winter sun, a beautiful dawn, a ray of light, a moonlit night. She was, in short, a veritable miracle. The same decade, however, also saw the release of *Andaz* (produced by Pahlaj Nihalani) in which Juhi Chawla's character describes herself as a *maal gaadi* that needs – ahem – a bit of *dhakka lagana*, as she euphemistically eggs on her husband (played by Anil Kapoor) to go at it. The song was constructed around the principles of rail locomotives and its lyrics described the pistons doing their job at slow and fast paces to enable the train to reach its destination. Not Hindi cinema's greatest poetic achievement, for sure.

The final part of the romance was obviously the separation. A separation has traditionally been associated with tears (for both involved), alcohol (mostly shown as a male indulgence), black streaks of kohl running across the cheeks (for the female) and dishevelled hair (again for both). In *Sahib Bibi aur Ghulam*, however, it was the woman in the relationship who took to alcohol on being abandoned by her man. When Chhoti Bahu's husband prepared to leave for his tryst with another woman, she plaintively sang, 'Na jao saiyyan, chhudake baiyyaan, kasam tumhari main ro padoongi'. The song was about her status as his slave in love, desperate for his attention and determined to remain steadfastly at his feet. That the character was played by Hindi cinema's designated tragedy queen Meena Kumari was a significant feature of the carefully constructed tableau of grief caused by abandonment.

Cut to 1987. In *Ijaazat*, the woman was still shaken at the separation from her man but some modern elements had crept in. First, it was not a marriage but a relationship. Second, the woman, though distraught, was not asking the man to come back to her. She was asking instead for her 'things' – her memories and their moments of togetherness – to be returned to her.

'Mera kuch saman tumhare pass padha hai,' she sang, and counted among the things she wanted back wet, rainy days, moonlit nights, the smell of fresh mehendi on her palms and even some false promises. By the time another three decades had gone by, the woman seemed to have figured out quite completely how to cope with parting from her partner. In *Ae Dil Hai Mushkil*, Alizeh (Anushka Sharma) had got over her man completely – or, at least, appeared to have figured out what she needed to do to get over him. 'Dil pe patthar rakhke mooh pe make-up kar liya,' she sang, listing spa therapy, girlfriend therapy and party therapy as the natural steps to take while getting over a broken relationship.

**Songs of Patriotism**

After Independence, it was imperative that the nation's self-confidence be rebuilt if development and self-sufficiency were to be brought about. The main theme of patriotic songs in the films that were released in the years following 1947 was the grand showcasing of our braves, our farmers, our monuments, our geographic splendour, our rich heritage, and so on. Be it 'Yeh desh hai veer jawanon ki' (*Naya Daur*) or 'Nanha munna rahi hoon' (*Son of India*, 1962) or the hyper-popular 'Mere desh ki dharti sona ugle' (*Upkar*, 1967), each song was about what India had to offer.

There were also songs that had patriots pledging their commitment to the cause of the country. In *Karma*, heroes, heroines, character actors, junior artistes – all followers of different religions – sang, 'Dil diya hai, jaan bhi denge ae watan tere liye,' and promised to fight for their country till the last drop of their blood. When confronted with terrorists burning the tricolour, a chubby computer engineer (Arvind Swamy) threw himself on the flames to protect the flag (*Roja*, 1992), the thumping tempo of 'Bharat humko jaan se pyara hai' playing in the background.

As the size of the Indian diaspora increased, a trend of people returning simultaneously developed, as though the most patriotic thing an able-bodied and able-minded Indian living abroad could do for the country was to return. 'Yeh jo des hai tera, swades hai tera' from *Swades* was about inspiring successful NRIs to give up their comfortable lives abroad and return to their roots. The draw of the country was no longer the lush green fields (useless for city slickers!) or the grand spectacle of the Taj Mahal (who was going to negotiate those long queues at the entrance?) as promised in earlier songs, but the simple fact that it was home. Did it work? Well, reverse brain drain has been a much-observed and debated phenomenon of the last decade!

## Songs of Flight

The portrayal of patriotism in cinema had begun in the context of the freedom movement, but symbols of freedom exist in many different forms in Hindi cinema – the most common one being the desire to fly. Yet, even this simple, almost childish desire has been depicted differently over the years. In *Chori Chori* (1956), Nargis playing the typical sheltered, rich brat, sang, 'Panchhi banoo, udti phiroon mast gagan mein' and of how buoyant she felt 'duniya ke chaman mein'. In *Seeta aur Geeta*, Hema Malini and Sanjeev Kumar played out the closest approximation of flying on flat ground when they rolled around on skates singing, 'Hawa ke saath saath, ghata ke sang sang', pretending to be among the winds and clouds. They were in love, and love had made them feel light and uplifted. In *Jo Jeeta Wohi Sikandar*, Aamir Khan described his experience of falling in love for the first time through much the same imagery in the smashing song 'Udta hi phiroon in hawaon mein kahin, ya main jhool jaoon in ghataon mein kahin.'

But not all songs that have flight as the central image have been about a joyous feeling. When the angst-ridden wannabe-musician Janardhan Jakhar (Ranbir Kapoor) took off from his home in *Rockstar* (2011), he sang, 'Phir se udd chala, udd ke chhoda hai jahan neeche'. His flight, however, was not towards a bright future (well, it was, but he wasn't aware of it then); rather, he was escaping the memory of his beloved becoming someone else's wife. The jilted lover was hardly a new thing in Hindi cinema at the time, but the use of the imagery of flight to denote sorrow definitely was. It is an image that is likely to return again and again as films increasingly portray the trials and travails of modern lives.

### Songs of Prayer

Since the advent of Hindi films, songs of gratitude, prayer, supplication and adoration have been dedicated to a higher being, so much so that the prayer song can be categorized as a full-fledged genre in Hindi films.

The group of reforming criminals in *Do Aankhen Barah Hath* (1957) came together in prayer, singing, 'Ae maalik, tere bande hum', a song that proclaimed complete devotion to the Almighty in the face of the burdens and misfortunes of human life. Much later in *The Burning Train*, faith remained in full force as a train hurtled towards its fiery fate and a group of children, facing certain death, hailed the Almighty as the master of all he surveys and praised him for his generosity, 'Tera hi zameen tera aasmaan, tu bada meherbaan tu bakshish kar.' A more positive version of the prayer song, 'Hum ko mann ki shakti dena', featured in *Guddi* (1971) a song sung by school children at their morning assembly, asking God to grant the will to be courageous, righteous and sincere towards oneself and others.

Over the years, the songs addressed to gods in our films have become less serious, and more playful and even borrowed from the Bhakti traditions of looking upon god with affection and love. In *Jhankaar Beats* (2003), 'Tu aashiqui hai' was performed in church like a gospel song and God was proclaimed to be the amalgamation of love, happiness and shelter, as the journey as well as the destination. In *Rab Ne Bana De Jodi* (2008), it was the beloved who became the embodiment of God when Shah Rukh Khan sang, 'Tujh mein rab dikhta hai, yaara main kya karoon'. An inclusive vision indeed!

## Songs Dedicated to 'Papa'

In the early Hindi films, the father was referred to as an incarnation of god. Most songs dedicated to the father hailed him as the granter of blessings, especially as tearful daughters left for their marital homes. 'Babul ki duayein leti jaa' from *Neelkamal* (1968) or 'O babul pyare' from *Johny Mera Naam* (1970) focused on the tenderness of the father-daughter relationship, their sorrow at parting from each other expressed in suitably plaintive tones.

By the 1980s, the father was portrayed as more of a friend. His dreams and ambitions for his children were taken as points of inspiration and aspiration, as Aamir Khan's character so charmingly expressed in the lyrics of 'Papa kehte hain bada naam karega' (*Qayamat Se Qayamat Tak*). 'Tu mera dil, tu meri jaan' from *Akele Hum Akele Tum* (1995) portrayed a very special relationship between a single father and his son. They were pals, each other's support, their lives inextricably entwined.

In 2016, another Aamir Khan film (*Dangal*) marked a further transition with a perfectionist father being demonized by his exhausted, despairing children with the words, 'Bapu, sehat ke liye tu toh hanikaarak hai'. The daughters' affection and respect for the father had transcended into a completely different emotion altogether!

## The Boat Song

Another genre of Hindi film songs – the boat song – was usually employed to depict journeys, both physical and emotional. The template for the boat song was first depicted in *Bandini*, when a minstrel at the riverside sang addressed the boatman with, 'O re majhi, mere saajan hai us paar', singing of the uncertainty of a union with the beloved, a niggling doubt about the very presence of the lover across the river. This particular boat song was about a journey, but it was not one of hope. S.D. Burman's unusual voice – neither romantic nor tragic, just different – added to the feeling of uncertainty that the song evoked. Most avid listeners would say they didn't know what to expect at the end of it. The boat song in *Khushboo* (1975), 'O maajhi re', on the other hand, was about finding shelter and support for oneself as the boat ride took the protagonist across a river – literally and metaphorically.

But that was before the confident youth of liberalized India jumped on to a boat himself and co-opted his friends for a grand ride. In *Kaho Naa Pyaar Hai* (2000), Hrithik Roshan's character sang 'Pyar ki kashti mein, lehron ki masti mein' as he swung from the cruise boat's sails, his fan-friends happily following his every move. No longer was there any uncertainty about the crossing, the other side or the person waiting there – on this boat dreams came true and true love was easily found.

(While on the subject of boat songs, 'O majhi' from *Bandhe Haath* [1973] needs to be mentioned. This Amitabh Bachchan-Mumtaz number – ostensibly a 'boat song' – was performed as a cabaret. While the lyrics of the song were exactly in the mould of requesting the boatman for help in crossing the river, in the hands of the maverick music-maker R.D. Burman it was sung, and performed, to the tune of a slinky dance number!)

## The Cabaret

The cabaret is essentially a European form of entertainment featuring music, dance, recitation or drama and is exclusively performed at pubs, restaurants or night clubs with a table-seated audience enjoying dinner or drinks. Initially, the cabaret was featured in Hindi films as 'club' numbers playing on its choice of venue and has slowly morphed into what is today known as the 'item number'. Originally, it was a dance that was performed specifically by vamps, but as heroines became bolder they too performed cabaret numbers. The cabaret in Hindi cinema usually portrays a cesspool that the hero is being drawn into or the den of vice that the villain is running. The standard cabaret sequence involved someone getting drunk in a psychedelically lit bar as a scantily clad beauty belted out a jazzy song with suitably energetic dance moves.

Helen – almost always the purveyor-in-chief of the aforementioned vices through the 1970s and 1980s – performed these songs with gusto and lured menfolk into her world. If one has to select a cabaret song from among the ones featuring Helen, one would choose 'O mungda mungda, main gud ki dali' from *Inkaar* (1977). While it came towards the end of Helen's career, it perfectly depicts the temptress within the scenario of alcohol, gambling and assorted evils that these songs sought to show. As with almost all these songs, the lyrics were squarely about the woman's ability to be the centre of attraction as a seductress, offering intoxication to all those who came to her: 'Zara mera nasha bhi chakh le aaya jo meri gali / Mangta hai toh aaja rasiya nahin toh main yeh chali…'

The confidence of the seductress that these songs conveyed has not changed with time. When Sunny Leone blazed the screens in *Ragini MMS 2* (2014) and crooned 'Baby doll main sone di', she was supremely confident about her value as the golden doll of sass in a world made of brass.

From the 1960s to the 2000s, the lyrics have changed from Hindi to Punjabi; the performer has become a tad bolder in her choice of clothing; and the visuals of male supplication to this earthly goddess are more pronounced. But it is still a den of evil she is being willingly followed into. In short, the cabaret is alive and kicking!

### The Fairness Song

I can't really call this last selection a category. It is, however, an interesting pointer to an unhealthy obsession among the majority of Indians. *Baharon ke Sapne* (1967) had a song with lyrics like 'Aaja piya tohe pyaar doon, gori baiyan tohe vaar doon' in which a woman used her 'fair wrists' to express her love. This is not an aberration. A large number of songs have used the term *gori* to symbolize beauty and it's difficult to think of another Hindi word that is used this prolifically to describe a beautiful woman.

*Chitchor*'s 'Gori tera gaon bada pyara', *Roti*'s 'Gore rang pe na itna gumaan kar' or *Aaj ka Arjun*'s 'Gori hain kalaiyan' have all steadfastly focused on fairness of the skin to express admiration for the woman. One of the worthies in this list was the wonderfully catchy 'Chittiyaan kalaiyaan' from *Roy* (2015) – yet another ode to pale wrists – the lyrics of which harked back to a time when a woman used to be covered from head to toe, and the poet (or her admirer) could only see her (fair) wrists for inspiration to compose his odes. In *Roy*, however, actress Jacqueline Fernandes flaunts her fair wrists (along with her flowing hair, shapely figure and energetic dance moves) just to cajole her man to take her shopping and film watching.

You could say the words have changed – from *gori* to *chitti*. Or you could say that the more things change, the more they remain the same. The preoccupation with fairness of the skin may be unwarranted and unwanted, but it looks like it's here to stay.

### Ten songs for the starry-eyed

**'Chaudhvin ka chand ho, ya aftab ho'** from *Chaudhvin ka Chand* (1960)

**'Dhal gaya din, ho gayi sham'** from *Humjoli* (1970)

**'Phool baharon se nikla, chand sitaron se nikla… O mehbooba'** from *Sholay* (1975)

**'Jaadon ki narm dhoop aur aangan mein let kar… Dil dhoondta hai phir wohi phursat ke raat din'** from *Mausam* (1975)

**'Chand mera dil, chandni ho tum'** from *Hum Kisi Se Kum Nahin* (1977)

**'Dhoop mein nikla na karo roop ki rani'** from *Geraftaar* (1985)

**'Tum aaye to aaya mujhe yaad, gali mein aaj chand nikla'** from *Zakhm* (1999)

**'Sooraj hua maddham, chand jalne laga'** from *Kabhi Khushi Kabhie Gham* (2001)

**'Chanda mama so gaye, sooraj chachu jaage'** from *Munna Bhai MBBS* (2003)

**'Sooraj dooba hai yaaron, do ghoont nashe ke maaro'** from *Roy* (2015)

# 8

# WHAT IS YOUR STYLE NUMBER?

## HIGHLIGHTS OF FILMI FASHION

ON 12 DECEMBER 2008, WHEN ADITYA CHOPRA'S FILM *Rab Ne Bana Di Jodi*, with Shah Rukh Khan in the lead, released on thousands of screens across the country, audiences of the film at a particular multiplex were greeted by staff with their hair cropped really short and designs running across the scalp where the hair had been shaved down to the skin. It turned out that the Aamir Khan-starrer *Ghajini* was to be released two weeks later, and the film's marketing team had managed to convince the employees of the multiplex to cut their hair like Aamir's character in the film. They had thus become walking-talking pre-release publicity machines for the film! The '*Ghajini* haircut' went on to become a rage as hundreds of people began to sport the (then) unusual style.

From haircuts to attire to accessories, Hindi cinema has very often defined fashion trends in India. While certain sections of society may have laughed at the kitschy quality of filmi fashion, the masses have – over decades – faithfully copied their favourite stars' hairstyle or choice of clothes or even their mannerisms. More recently, as top fashion designers have begun working for films, and film stars have emerged as fashion icons in their own right, even those less swayed by filmi fashion have succumbed to the glamour of it all. Dev Anand's flashy cravats were a thing in the 1960s; Ranbir Kapoor's graphic tees have started a trend now – and film stars still rule our wardrobes.

*

TO trace our way back to one of the earliest rages in filmi fashion, we need to go back to the days of *Mughal-e-Azam* (the film, not the emperor). Ever since the character of Anarkali appeared on screen (played with aplomb by the gorgeous Madhubala), she has been deemed a fashion diva. The makers of the film spent a tonne of money to create costumes of fine silk intricately embroidered with thread and zari to match the original clothes and ornaments worn by people of the Mughal era. Tailors from Delhi and jewellery artisans from Hyderabad were brought to Bombay to recreate the period's clothing. The standout piece among the costumes was a famous outfit worn by Madhubala– a long, flowing, voluminous kurta paired with a fitted churidar– that became immortalized as the 'anarkali'. Nearly sixty years after the film was made, the anarkali is still an extremely popular cut for kurtas and dresses for women. (I've always felt this to be an interesting dilemma. We know that clothing of the particular cut existed during the Mughal era, but we don't know for sure if Anarkali herself existed – and even today we refer to a fictional character when asking for a real piece of clothing.)

*

HAVING acted in a Sindhi film, Sadhna Shivdasani was spotted in a film magazine by Sashadhar Mukherjee and selected for his production, *Love in Shimla* (1960), a dream debut by any standards. Except, in the judgemental world of Hindi cinema, where the heroine's appearance could sometimes decide the fate of a film, her wide forehead was seen to be a problem. When a strip of hair affixed to her forehead didn't work as a temporary solution, Sadhna opted for a haircut inspired by Audrey Hepburn. She soon appeared in a few high-profile films (like *Waqt*, 1965 and *Woh Kaun Thi?*, 1964) and her new hairstyle became popular across the country. Women of all ages wore the 'Sadhna cut. Beauty parlours of the 1960s and 1970s had photos of Sadhna pinned on their walls to encourage potential customers to choose the look. Long after Sadhna has retired from acting the 'Sadhna cut' remains an easy way to describe bangs covering a part of the forehead.

*

ONE of the most versatile actresses of her time, Sharmila Tagore made her acting debut in Satyajit Ray's *Apur Sansar* (1959), wrapped in a sari whose pallu covered her head to fit the part of a young, demure Bengali bride. Her debut Hindi film, *Kashmir Ki Kali* (1964), had her playing the role of a charming Kashmiri flower-seller clad in the traditional salwar-kameez and phiran. A few years later, in 1967, Tagore, still in her early-twenties, burst on to the screen in *An Evening in Paris* wearing a blue swimsuit. This probably came as less of a shock because the previous year the country had ogled in slack-jawed amazement when Sharmila Tagore had posed for *Filmfare* magazine in a bikini. The story goes that she had walked into the studio for the shoot with just a handbag , and when the photographer asked about her costumes for the shoot she patted her bag and assured him that she had everything she needed!

In the 1960s, the bikini was not an item of clothing that could be imitated widely in India and, naturally, it didn't fuel a fashion revolution. But it suddenly (and certainly) shook up not just the filmi fashion scene but the country as a whole. Tagore's bold statement got our stodgy political leaders raising the issue of vulgarity in the Parliament and heated debates ensued all around. Soon, Hindi films went back to portraying vamps and 'modern women' in dresses (or cabaret costumes) and the lead female characters in sarees. For decades, the bikini remained a piece of clothing associated with scandal and outrage. Even in the 2000s, heroines wearing bikinis (Sharmila Tagore's daughter-in-law, Kareena Kapoor, for example) still trigger breathless media coverage.

*

TALKING about sarees, if you search on YouTube for '*Brahmachari* Mumtaz song', what comes up is the sequence Mumtaz performed to: 'Aajkal tere mere pyar ke charche har zabaan par...', shimmying in a glittery bright orange saree wrapped tightly around her. Along with it, you'll be served up a bunch of suggestions of do-it-yourself videos on how to drape a saree in exactly the same way that Mumtaz had done for the song, each registering lakhs of views. This particular style is a hot favourite for another reason – experts recommend it as the drape to adopt to make oneself look slimmer. Mumtaz wasn't the usual demure Hindi film heroine. She was a quite the fashion icon and played her roles with considerable chutzpah. And look at how popular she still is!

*

RAJESH Khanna was not *a* superstar; he was *the* superstar. Everything he did or said ended up being copied by millions of his fans across the country. His slightly unusual sartorial style included pairing short kurtas with slim-fit trousers. The kurtas had what was popularly known as the 'guru collar', with a round neck and short, button plackets under the upright collar. He wore one in dapper style in *Kati Patang* (1971), for instance, and it became so popular that his designers – Stylo Tailors – were besieged by fans who came to them with photographs of the star, wanting their clothes to be stitched in exactly the same way as his – from the material used down to every last button. Rajesh Khanna's fan following didn't end in the 1970s. The 'guru collar' is still very popular and pops up often enough in fashion circles. Not bad for a man who got upstaged by a contemporary whose on-screen image had very little to do with his clothes.

*

THIS, of course, was Amitabh Bachchan, who broke into the top rung of the industry with such roles that required his clothes to be more torn and dirty than anything else. Over time, as Bachchan's popularity grew, more than the clothes he wore it was his persona that became the object of imitation. His signature clothes in many memorable films such as *Don* (1978) – the shirts with wide collars and bell-bottom trousers – became massively popular, and so did his mannerisms. The passion that Amitabh Bachchan roused among his legion of fans was depicted in *Gangs of Wasseypur Part 1*, in which Nawazuddin Siddiqui's character modelled his hair, his clothes, his sunglasses and even his walk on Bachchan's – as did thousands of his fans over decades. This part of *Gangs of Wasseypur* was set in the mid-1990s, indicating how trends in filmi fashion endure, especially in India's small towns. One of Amitabh Bachchan's most famous costumes was the coolie's uniform he wore in *Deewaar*. The knotted-at-the-hip blue shirt and khaki trousers became a rage like no other. Many years later, Bachchan clarified that his look in the film was not intentional but that he had had to knot his shirt because the one that was stitched for him turned out to be too long. (Which, of course, begs a curious question about the tailor who managed to stitch a shirt that was too long for the country's tallest actor!).

*

TRENDS are not set by actors alone. Sometimes the makers of the film too make a style statement by using the actors as their models and films as their ramps.

With his unusual take on love, the luscious locales in which his films were set and the rich quality of cinematography, legendary director and producer Yash Chopra was known as the king of romance. His formula for the hugely popular films he produced had one more key ingredient – his cast was always clothed like a dream. Glamorous clothing was central to his films from the beginning of his career, but it was only when he released the heroine-centric *Chandni* (1989) that it became something of a trademark. In the film, Sridevi, in the title role, wore a variety of knockout chiffon sarees – the most well-known among them being the slinky, yellow number she wore in a song sequence shot on the grand meadows of Switzerland. If Raj Kapoor was known for featuring 'women in white' in his films, Yash Chopra's films now became about the 'women in chiffons'. While Yash Chopra did show chiffon-clad heroines in several films, it was his avid admirers – film-makers like Karan Johar and Farah Khan – who cemented the image further through their tributes to him in their own films. In Farah Khan's debut film *Main Hoon Na* (2004), Sushmita Sen's character – always dressed in brightly coloured shimmering chiffons – was introduced as a tribute to Yash Chopra. Her name in the film was Chandni Chopra.

*

WHEN Madhuri Dixit featured on the cover of *India Today* magazine as the 'Star of the '90s' in September 1993, the cover image showed her dressed in a purple brocade saree and backless blouse ensemble. This would have been unremarkable if the release of her biggest blockbuster, *Hum Aapke Hain Koun..!*, in which the particular outfit featured, hadn't been one year away. The general response to the cover – so apt for a cover story that explored Madhuri's appeal among different sections of the audience – was prescient of the craze that the ensemble would become. A love story set against the backdrop of a big fat Indian wedding, the film was like an extended video recording of a real wedding and the costumes worn in it inspired a million clones. Wedding seasons, Diwali parties and even karwa chauth evenings across north and west India were never complete without women in wearing the ensembles that were a perfect mix of sexy and *sanskari*.

*

WITH the entry of top fashion designers into the costumes and styling department of Hindi films in the late 1980s and into the 1990s, filmi fashion got a cool twist. Film clothing started becoming more in sync with the times and distinctly more urban – probably in line with the audience now being concentrated in the cities and towns. When Manish Malhotra designed the clothes for Kareena Kapoor's carefree Geet in *Jab We Met* (2007), the result was quite far removed from the haute couture we are used to seeing in his fashion shows. In the film, Kareena played the typical girl-next-door – a bubbly, supremely talkative one – and for a large part of the film, she was dressed in long white tee-shirts paired with Patiala salwars. All of Kareena's clothes in the film were cool, comfortable and accessible, which the public seemed to love, but the Patiala-and-tee combo was the biggest hit. The long, loose, flowing combination – ideal for sleeping – suddenly came out of the bedroom and was in fashion stores everywhere. (Incidentally, the *Mughal-e-Azam* poster print on her tee-shirt in the film is proof enough of the enduring influence of Anarkali from *Mughal-e-Azam*, much beyond the style and length of the eponymous outfit.)

*

WHILE the clothes and mannerisms of the film stars have been emulated by fans, very rarely does a personal accessory of a film star become a fashion statement, let alone a part of her or his on-screen persona. It takes a star of some stature to reach this level. But then, Salman Khan is not your regular film star. He is 'Bhai' to probably the biggest and most loyal fan base seen in a very long time. Salman Khan has been wearing a bracelet with a *firoza* (turquoise) stone from around

2003. His father Salim Khan used to wear a similar bracelet and Salman is said to have got it copied. It became his lucky charm after successive films became blockbuster hits right after he started wearing it. The bracelet has featured in several of his films (those in which 'it doesn't clash with his on-screen character'), like *Tere Naam* (2003), *Partner*, *Ready* (2011) and, most famously, *Jai Ho* (2014), in which the scene that introduced him featured the bracelet prominently. As is the norm with most things Salman does, the moment his fans noticed the bracelet, Mumbai's roadside stalls, online shopping sites and faux-jewellery shops started stocking it at various price points! Incidentally, another accessory worn by Salman – the mace locket he wore around his neck in *Bajrangi Bhaijaan* (2015) – also became a runaway bestseller immediately after it went on sale on Amazon. The massive sale of the locket is one of the very few examples of official merchandise of a Hindi film becoming a commercial success.

*

FROM hairstyles to trousers, caps to shoes, jewellery to accessories, Hindi cinema has defined the fashion consciousness of this country – for better or for worse. Youngsters wearing *Maine Pyar Kiya*'s FRIEND cap look cute while potbellied middle-aged men sporting Hrithik Roshan's figure-hugging tee-shirts are a sight you wouldn't wish upon your worst enemy. Either way, it is a ringing endorsement of Hindi cinema as a force of social change, at least, when it comes to the clothes.

## Ten songs that wore it light

**Shoes, trousers, hat:** 'Mera joota hai Japani, yeh patloon Inglistani, sar pe lal topi Russi, phir bhi dil hai Hindustani' (*Shree 420*)

**Silk, netted salwar kurta:** 'Reshmi salwar kurta jali ka' (*Naya Daur*)

**Jhumkas:** 'Jhumka gira re, Bareilly ke bazaar mein' (*Mera Saaya*)

**Suit and boots befitting a Londoner:** 'Saala main toh sahab ban gaya, yeh suit mera dekho, yeh boot mera dekho, jaise gora koi London ka' (*Sagina*)

**Tilted hat:** 'Tirchi topiwale, O babu bhole bhale' (*Tridev*)

**Red dupatta, black kurta:** 'O lal dupattewali tera naam toh bata, o kaale kurtewali tera naam toh bataa' (*Aankhen*)

**Green dupatta:** 'Dulhe ki saaliyon, o hare dupatte waliyon' (*Hum Aapke Hain Koun..!*)

**Rado watches, Gucci perfumes:** 'Rado ki ghadi haathon mein, perfume Gucci wala, but Pappu can't dance saala' (*Jaane Tu Yaa Jaane Na*)

**Clothes from Sarojini Nagar market** (Delhi's leading destination for budget shoppers)**:** 'Sarojini ke kapde pehen ke jaati madam disco' (*Humpty Sharma Ki Dulhania*)

**The traditional salwar–kameez:** 'Tenu suit suit karda' (*Hindi Medium*)

# 9

# TERI MERI KAHAANI

## BOLLYWOOD BIOPICS

PUBLIC FIGURES ARE RARELY PREPARED TO OR INCLINED to reveal much about their private lives. They either refuse access or control the narrative in exchange for access. Biopics, therefore, tend to operate on a schizophrenic scale, ranging from saccharine-sweet hagiography to warts-and-all depictions that attract court cases. In Hindi cinema, though, biographies usually fall into the former category, steering clear of obvious negative references and sometimes produced in the guise of fiction to avoid legal hassles – these may be dramatic, but they are neither real nor insightful. Biopics that are 'authorized' are usually too sanitized and one-sided.

When it comes to Hindi cinema, biopics have been around for fairly long, covering a wide range of subjects and produced in varied treatments and styles to deftly dodge legal action from the subject's family, the wrath of the subject's followers and undesirable attention from outrage-happy groups. They seem to have gained more popularity in recent times, with a slew of interesting personalities as their subjects. Mature handling of sensitive material, though, is unfortunately still quite rare.

**Freedom Fighters**

India's 200-year-long freedom struggle has a long list of iconic as well as forgotten figures whose bravery and exploits have been eminently film-worthy. Before 1947, films could not be based on real freedom fighters because of censorship issues, but the years after Independence saw several of them being produced. While many subjects were explored, Bollywood's favourite revolutionary so far has turned out to be – without a shade of doubt – Bhagat Singh. The young Sikh revolutionary who disguised himself by shaving off his beard and dropping his turban, his Avengers-like team that fought for freedom, his final act of daredevilry (bombing the Central Legislative Assembly), and his fiery ideology and messages have been fodder for many a star vehicle: Shammi Kapoor and Manoj Kumar during the 1960s, and Ajay Devgn, Bobby Deol and Sonu Sood, all in 2002, have played the revolutionary.

While the films followed the broad flow of political

events that occurred during Bhagat Singh's lifetime, they were largely glamorized for cinematic purposes. For instance, *23 March 1931: Shaheed* had Bobby Deol playing the young revolutionary, while *The Legend of Bhagat Singh* starred Ajay Devgn, but these films also had Aishwarya Rai and Amrita Rao respectively appearing as the freedom fighter's girlfriend – a character that the films could have well done without. Romantic dalliances were after all contrary to the life's message of a revolutionary who claimed freedom to be his bride. (On the other hand, *Rang De Basanti*, which released in 2006, had an interesting take on Bhagat Singh. In it, the life of a cynical, modern-day college student co-opted to play the freedom fighter in a documentary slowly unravels as the ideals of the past and the character he is playing takes over his present.)

Wives and girlfriends of freedom fighters are touchy subjects among India's audiences. Unlike Bhagat Singh, who did not have a relationship in real life, Subhash Chandra Bose – the other firebrand freedom fighter – had a legally wedded wife, with whom he had a daughter. But when Shyam Benegal's *Netaji Subhas Chandra Bose: The Forgotten Hero* (2005) released, there were protests against the depiction of his private life. Fortunately, the marriage had a very small part to play in the film's story and Benegal had done enough research to defend his work against the allegations.

Benegal, who has made several biopics, (some of which are listed later in the chapter) made a point relevant for all biopics in India. In an interview at the time of release of the 2005 film, he said, 'There are no trained people to deal with period films, and you have to look into everything yourself and that is the most exhausting part of making a period film. In the West, you could just buy the support, here you spend a lot of time putting things together.' That is why, perhaps, many film-makers just make do with a 'based on true events' disclaimer added to a biopic's credits (and then invent a love interest so they may insert a potential 'hit' song).

**Politicians**

One man's freedom fighter is his children's politician. When Independence dawned, the idealism that people had strived for through years of struggle and oppression started fading and the khadi-clad people who had been elected as leaders began to fail those who had chosen them as representatives. The years during which Jawaharlal Nehru helmed the nation were marked by idealism but soon corruption crept in at the topmost levels – and cynicism at the bottom of the pyramid. When this cynicism was its peak, Gulzar's *Aandhi* released and caused a massive storm. It was a seemingly innocuous story about an ambitious woman who leaves her husband to pursue a career in politics. As she comes back to campaign in her home town, she meets her estranged husband and remembers their love story. So far, so good. Then came what the *Times of India* called 'an awkward distraction…perhaps no part of the original story…only coincidental to the film'. The politician had a widely recognizable streak of white in her otherwise dark hair and her dressing and demeanour were almost identical to the most famous politician in the country at the time – who also happened to be the prime minister. *Aandhi* can hardly be called Indira Gandhi's biopic, but the furore raised over allegations that it was eventually led to the film being banned after the Emergency was declared in the year of its release. The controversy took a clearly fictional film (which, some say, was actually based on the life of the then chief minister of Orissa, Nandini Satpathy) and pushed it firmly into the genre of biopics.

One of Hindi cinema's better efforts was its retelling of the story of Sardar Vallabhbhai Patel – India's first deputy prime minister and home minister – is much more interesting when one comes to his years as a politician than when he was a freedom fighter. Ketan Mehta's *Sardar* (1993) did a fine job of chronicling the life and times of the man who could have become India's first prime minister. Paresh Rawal brilliantly played the title role of Patel, who went from being a Gandhihating Anglophile to the grand old man who literally unified India after communal tensions threatened to tear the country apart. This film was in the best traditions of a biopic – historically accurate, anecdotally rich and perfect in terms of casting. But in the absence of trademark Hindi film songs and sufficiently jingoistic screaming, it did not garner the interest and admiration that it deserved.

### Agents of Social Change

Just before the release of *Toilet: Ek Prem Katha* (2017), Anita Narre of Madhya Pradesh – on whom the film is allegedly based – refused to grant the producers permission to release the film unless she was given a share of the film's profits. Her bold exit from her marital home because it didn't have a toilet had made her a bona fide change agent, though the incident left a slightly bitter taste in the mouth. But this episode can be counted as an exception because, by and large, social change agents are easier subjects to film. The stories of how they came to initiate movements and what pushed them to succeed can be tremendously dramatic. Also since, they are usually eager to spread their message, they tend to be more open to cooperating with the film-makers along the way.

One of the earliest films made in this vein was based on Dwarkanath Kotnis. A freshly minted medical graduate, he was deputed to go to China in 1938 as a part of an Indian mission to help the Chinese during the Second Sino-Japanese War. A part of Mao Zedong's army, he was always at the front and treated soldiers for long hours with little access to medicines and other supplies. Kotnis married a Chinese nurse and had a son with her, but died prematurely due to ill-health caused by his line of work. Film-maker V. Shantaram and writer K.A. Abbas believed this would make a gripping story and, just three years after the doctor's death, they made *Dr Kotnis ki Amar Kahani* (1946). Shantaram played the title role himself and the film had strong nationalist rhetoric. Since Congress stalwarts like Jawaharlal Nehru and Subhas Chandra Bose were instrumental in organizing the mission to China, the producers also wanted to seek the blessings of the Indian National Congress to promote the film. Although that did not eventually come through, the film still managed to turn its hero into a popular name in the country. (Dr Kotnis was already a hero in China.) As a biopic, it was neither 'authorized' nor was there any clarity on the inputs sought from the subject's family. But that may have proved to be irrelevant as the story was well-known, and the focus was on Dr Kotnis's nationalism and not his personal life.

Another such figure to be immortalized on the silver screen was Amul's Dr Verghese Kurien. The first words of the credits of the film *Manthan* were: '500,000 farmers of Gujarat present...' The film was not only based on the life of Dr Kurien but he was also the driving force behind it. Shyam Benegal had previously made two documentaries on his Operation Flood movement but told Dr Kurien that only a feature film would succeed in reaching those who were unconvinced about the movement. Since there were no funds for the film, Dr Kurien stepped in and told all the members of his cooperative to take two rupees less for one packet of milk they sold. The five lakh members indeed did so, and *Manthan* became India's first crowdfunded film. The film credits Dr Kurien for the idea behind the story and takes a snapshot from his life – how he set up the first milk cooperative and took the first step towards Gujarat's milk revolution. As Benegal had promised, the film was not a propaganda reel but showed both the villagers and the Dairy Board personnel as real people with strengths and weaknesses, creating a gripping narrative that didn't shy away from addressing the issues of feudalism, caste and poverty. The result was a film that turned Dr Kurien into a hero and its half a million producers into trailblazers.

### Gangsters

What is the worst that can happen if your subject doesn't like the biopic you make? In Mumbai, the answer can be quite alarming, what with the underworld dons having a history of dispatching from this earth film-makers who do not agree to do their bidding. In fact, this is probably the primary reason for films creating larger-than-life, heroic gangsters with sympathetic back stories who pursue altruistic activities on the side.

One of the best examples of this is Haji Mastan. Originally Mastan Haider Mirza, he began as a coolie at Bombay's Mazgaon docks who supplemented his meagre salary by smuggling imported transistors and watches. When he came across a gang of Pathans who were extorting protection money from his fellow coolies, Mastan got together a band of ten men, confronted the smaller gang of Pathans and beat them to a pulp. This story became a legend on screen when a dockyard coolie called Vijay Verma single-handedly took on a gang of extorting goons. It must be said that, although the story of Amitabh Bachchan-starrer *Deewaar* did have some similarities to the life of Haji Mastan, it can't be called a biopic by any stretch of the imagination.

On the other hand, *Once Upon a Time in Mumbaai* (2010) could possibly qualify as Mastan's biopic with Ajay Devgn playing Sultan Mirza, who rose from the docks to become a benevolent don with political ambitions – much like the man who inspired the role. The film had a one-plus-one offer for those curious about the underworld as it showed a ruthless ganglord

(Emraan Hashmi) beginning to emerge from behind the shadow of the older don. The character resembled Dawood Ibrahim, though in reality he had not been Haji Mastan's protégé. Dawood Ibrahim is one of the most featured gangsters in Hindi cinema, being portrayed in turn as heroic (*Company*), non-judgmental (*D*) and villainous (*D-Day*). Each of these films focused on one aspect of his life and suitably embellished it. *D* showed his rise from being a police constable's son to a small-time don and his liaison with a film actress. *Company* traced his journey as an international don, the running of his operations from his base abroad and his falling out with his main partner. *D-Day* showed him to be an ISI stooge, ensconced in Karachi but not fully immune to assassination attempts. However, all these films tread the ground carefully, keeping their stories fictional and vague in order to avoid the don's wrath.

An official or authorized biopic of a gangster seemed rather impossible to pull off for obvious reasons, till director Ashim Ahluwalia and actor Arjun Rampal produced *Daddy* (2017), based on the life of Arun Gawli. While speaking about the film's journey, Arjun Rampal – who was a co-writer on the film – said that it took him nearly three years to convince Gawli to give them permission to make the film the way they wanted to instead of by glorifying him. Though the treatment of the film betrayed a certain degree of admiration for Gawli, it showed his milieu and motivations fairly honestly. The film called him 'the one who didn't run', alluding to the other dons who had left India to escape the law. To prepare for his role, Arjun Rampal met several people in Dagdi Chawl (Gawli's den) – from Gawli's rival gangs to the cops who chased him – to get to the heart of the gangster's story. Eventually, all of them contributed to the final script. What started as an act of documentation for him as an actor ultimately became a major part of the script. Eschewing standard tropes of gangster films, like bombastic dialogue, item numbers performed in the hideouts of villains and heart-thumping chase scenes, the film was true to life but also managed to placate its subject by portraying him heroically enough.

**Policemen**

If there are gangsters it is only natural that cops will not be far behind.

One of the most dramatic and controversial episodes of law enforcement in India is the concept of the encounter killing. The extra-judicial killing of under-trial convicts has been debated to death after a fairly large posse of policemen – mostly in Mumbai – were accused of killing convicts they should or could have arrested. The debate pitted the obvious illegality of the killings against the toothless justice system, which was likely to have eventually set many of the criminals free. The media gleefully reported the body count that could be pinned on these officers, talked about their rivalry to reach 'milestones' and projected them as vigilantes providing justice. In *Shootout at Lokhandwala* (2007), a lawyer defending police officers accused of an encounter killing comes up with a practical yet amoral logic for the circumstances, 'There is a man with a gun standing outside your house. Would you rather that man is a policeman or a gangster?'

Arguably the most famous film on encounter killings is *Ab Tak Chhappan* (2004), allegedly based on India's most famous encounter cop, Daya Nayak. Shimit Amin directed Nana Patekar in this tight thriller about Special Branch cops going about dispensing their own brand of justice. The film was much more dramatic than the real-life incidents and the officer was built up as a larger-than-life hero doing his duty after being repeatedly let down by the system. There were more such films (like *Risk* [2007], *Department* [2012]) that were allegedly based on Inspector Nayak. In fact, there is a Telugu film called *Encounter Dayanayak* (2005). The spate of media and cinematic glorification stopped when many of the encounter specialists were accused of having underworld connections (and disproportionate incomes) and it was alleged that they killed gangsters on the basis of inputs and incentives from rival gangs.

Rakesh Maria, a legend in police circles in Mumbai, has been part some of the most high-profile investigations in the country. Being at the centre of showbiz has helped him get more exposure. Anupam Kher, for instance, played a Mumbai police commissioner in the film *A Wednesday* (2008) and said that he had spent some time with Maria to get his mannerisms right. But Kay Kay Menon, the person who actually played Rakesh Maria on screen in *Black Friday* (2007), Anurag Kashyap's film based on S. Husain Zaidi's book on the investigations into the 1993 Bombay blasts, didn't meet him as he claimed 'his persona could have overwhelmed me'. *Black Friday* was not a biopic of Rakesh Maria but a deep dive into what was probably his biggest case. Kay Kay Menon took inputs from Zaidi on the police officer and created such an intense character that it brought both him and Maria into the limelight. In an interview, Rakesh Maria has mentioned *Zanjeer* as one of the films that inspired him to become a policeman. With *Black Friday*, he probably became equated with his reel-life hero in real life!

**Filmstars**

Films on films are (reasonably) common and many of them have recognizable characters. *Luck by Chance* and *Om Shanti Om* (2007) are two films in which the walls between reel and real are broken because some characters play regular people while some real-life stars play themselves. On the other hand, *Khoya Khoya Chand* (2007) – based on the industry the way it was in the 1950s – is completely fictional but reminiscent of the lives of Guru Dutt and Waheeda Rehman.

A 'fictional' film but clearly based on an actor's life is Milan Luthria's *The Dirty Picture* (2011). It broke Vidya Balan free from her mould of the girl-next-door and set her on the path of bold, buxom stardom. (Apart from the film's massive commercial success, it got Vidya Balan the National Award for Best Actress.) Basing the film in the Tamil film industry of the 1970s and 1980s, it pieced together industry gossip, urban legends and news snippets to make a point about the objectification of women in films. *The Dirty Picture* also shows the interesting way in which unauthorized biopics operate. The film was initially proclaimed to be based on the life of the late sex-siren Silk Smitha till the star's family objected and sent a legal notice to the makers for not taking their permission before making the film. The producers (Balaji Pictures) then issued a statement saying that the film was not based on anybody's life in particular and '[drew] inspiration from the strugglers in 1980s whose indomitable spirit made them emerge triumphant'. Officially, that's where it stood. Unofficially, fans can chuckle at the fact that the film released on 2 December 2011 – which would have been Silk Smitha's 51st birthday.

The closest Hindi cinema has got to an official biopic of a film star's life (till now) is Shyam Benegal's *Bhumika* (1977). The film opened with two messages. The first one claimed that all characters in the film were fictitious but the second one said the film was 'inspired by *Sangty Aika* [in Marathi] by the late Hansa Wadkar'. This Marathi actress's brutally frank autobiography, highlighting the treatment of women in the film industry in particular and the world at large had created a big stir when it had released. A 22-year-old Smita Patil gave a virtuoso performance as the actress aging from teenage to middle-age on screen. The plot, the main characters and the background were all similar, if not identical, to the autobiography and one could say that the 'fiction' disclaimer was inserted to protect the film and its producers against any legal action by aggrieved persons.

In fact, Rajkumar Hirani's biopic on Sanjay Dutt (slated for release in 2018) will be the first truly official biopic of a filmstar. The script is an output of many, many hours of interviews the director conducted with the actor, and so far it seems that the actor is ready to show his chequered life in all its glory and ignominy. With Ranbir Kapoor playing Dutt and several major stars in key roles, this is likely to be one of the biggest 'true stories' of Hindi cinema.

**Sports Heroes**

Most of the rousing sports films in recent times have had the blessings of the subject, with many of them participating in the making and promotions of the films. In such a scenario, what differs is how the story unfolds on screen versus that in real life – sometimes changes are added for purposes of promoting a certain agenda or for dramatization. Thus, the stories are 'real' (read authorized) from the subject's point of view but claim to be fictional to avoid the ire of other characters. This also means that there is likely to be a fictitious rival, an imaginary spanner in the works, and some things that could have been true but aren't.

It is often said that *Chak De India* (2007) dramatized the story of Mir Ranjan Negi – India's hockey goalkeeper in a 1–7 loss against Pakistan in 1982. The film showed a Muslim forward missing a match-winning penalty against Pakistan, a far more egregious error than if it had been any other team, and then to compounding it by allowing the opposing team's captain to console him in a show of sportsmanship. The subsequent story of redemption – coaching the women's hockey team to win a Commonwealth Games gold in 2002 – also matched Negi's story. However, the scriptwriter, Jaideep

Sahni, said that his starting point was the victory of the women's team and that he initially had no idea of Negi's story. It was only when Negi came on board as a technical consultant that he read the script, started weeping and the crew realized the connection between him and the character to be played by Shah Rukh Khan. So here was a biopic that got made by accident!

This, though, is a rarity – sports biopics are often quite deliberate in choosing their subject. For instance, *Azhar* (2016) firmly placed India's disgraced cricket captain as the hero and approached the entire match-fixing issue from his – rather incredible – point of view. Azhar didn't fix matches. Azhar did take money from bookies but for good reason. Azhar took the bullet for others who were the real perpetrators. It went about disproving accusations of matches fixed by the cricketer by showcasing his batting performances, although always in other matches. Hindi film audiences have believed far more incredible things and they would probably have been more receptive of the film's premise if Azhar's role wasn't played by an actor (Emraan Hashmi) who had played a bookie in an earlier film (*Jannat*, 2008), which incidentally had been a hit!

*Dangal* is a biopic which is probably closest in reality to the real lives of its subjects. In the film, wrestler Mahavir Singh Phogat's quest to win an international gold through his daughters kept razor-sharp focus on his eldest daughter, Geeta, but in real life, his other daughters (Babita and Ritu) and nieces (Vinesh and Priyanka) are all international-level wrestlers. In fact, Babita won a silver at the same Commonwealth Games where her sister won a gold. *Dangal*'s deviations were inserted mainly to enhance the drama. Geeta Phogat's coach at the Sports Authority of India was in reality not the kind of man he was shown to be in the film. Her final bout to win gold was not a cliffhanger either, as she won quite easily in real life. Also, no one locked Mahavir Singh Phogat up in a room when his daughter was fighting for her gold. But the last fabrication can perhaps be forgiven because it helped create possibly the most rousing rendition of our national anthem in a Hindi film!

**Sensational Newsmakers**

These are biopic subjects who never wanted a biopic, because they were part of newspaper headlines that shouldn't have been.

Very seldom does a newspaper headline become popular enough to become a catchphrase. When the courts acquitted Manu Sharma of the murder of Jessica Lal, whom he murdered in the presence of more than a hundred witnesses, a headline in the *Times of India* screamed 'No One Killed Jessica'. The strong indictment of the judgement by the newspaper was enough for the media to take up the case as a cause and to warrant a full-blown film to be made with the phrase as a title. Sabrina Lal, Jessica Lal's sister (played on-screen by Vidya Balan), would be one of very few – if not the only – biopic subjects who unequivocally said that the film was a faithful version of her experiences. The central character in the film, played by Rani Mukerji, was an aggressive and principled reporter at the news channel NDTV. Given the prominence of the channel in the film, it was assumed that it was Barkha Dutt who was being portrayed but that's probably not true. For starters, most television channels – not just NDTV – took up the cause of seeking justice for Jessica. More importantly, the pivotal sting operation that exposed the witnesses who had lied was conducted by *Tehelka* magazine under journalist Harinder Baweja. But perhaps a magazine editor did not seem as glamorous as a television anchor to the makers of the film.

Biopics are usually made after an event is over or, often, when the subject is dead. The two biopics of Aarushi Talwar – both released in 2015 – forced the country to wake up to the fact that the principle of 'beyond reasonable doubt' hadn't been applied to the conviction of the murdered girl's under-trial parents. Meghna Gulzar's *Talvar* (2015) examined the process of the botched-up police investigation and the breathless media trial with an air of quiet exasperation. Irrfan, playing the investigating officer, was fantastic in his portrayal of the role as was the rest of cast who strongly underlined the unfairness of the way in which Talwars had been persecuted. Manish Gupta's *Rahasya* (2015), based on the same incident and its aftermath, had Kay Kay Menon in the lead and did a stellar job of presenting the same case but with a 'fiction' disclaimer. The Talwars filed a suit against *Rahasya* for 'distorting the facts of the case' but were unable to stop its release. The director of *Rahasya* claimed that *Talvar* was based on the Talwars' point of view on the case, and was hence completely biased in their favour. Irrespective of their individual slants, both films managed to raise the decibel level around the couple's unfair conviction based on inconclusive evidence. One could speculate that they had some impact – however tangential – on the subsequent acquittal of the Talwars. In that way, it would seem that it was the biopic that brought closure to the saga it was based on.

## Industrialists

Here's the thing – there is not a single official or authorized biopic on any industrialist in India. Not one.[5]

[5] A biopic of J.R.D. Tata has been in the making for quite some time though there is no sign of progress. The rumours doing the rounds say that John Abraham is keen on producing the film and acting in it.

Clearly, our captains of industry prefer to stay away from the limelight. The best-known fictional account of a businessman is *Guru* (2007), allegedly and loosely based on petroleum tycoon Dhirubhai Ambani. In the film, the key milestones of his life were recounted with minor changes while some characters and subplots were invented. At the end of it, a petrol pump attendant's meteoric rise to become the king of Indian stock markets is a story that held immense charm for every ordinary Indian. The film took some of the ethically dubious rumours surrounding Ambani's life and gave them a positive spin. His use of legal loopholes, evasion of excise duty, handling of politicians – practices that had been whispered about for years – were finally depicted on the big screen along with justifications on why they were necessary. The selection of these real incidents and urban legends from the senior Ambani's life was quite masterful – including a life-threatening cardiac arrest from which he came back almost miraculously (for the film's climax). The final speech denouncing the government's desire to suppress entrepreneurship was never delivered by the real man but one could argue it was the guiding principle of his business. (The film also depicted two idealistic men from the media, said to be based on stalwart journalists Ramnath Goenka and Arun Shourie.)

## Ordinary People, Extraordinary Circumstances

The extraordinary situations that citizens of this country face in their day-to-day lives tend to be quite depressing. Archaic laws. Apathetic bureaucracy. Crumbling infrastructure. Ineffective systems. And, occasionally, even crossfire. The by-product of these situations is the rise of heroes who sometimes win, sometimes succumb to the odds, but never really lose.

Director Tapan Sinha's *Ek Doctor Ki Maut* (1990) was based on the story of Dr Subhash Mukhopadhyay, who delivered India's first (and the world's second) child born by means of in-vitro fertilization (IVF). Instead of feting his achievement, the Indian government refused to acknowledge it, reprimanded him because he announced his feat to the media without taking their permission, and transferred him to a department where he couldn't follow up on his research. The concerted harassment led to the doctor committing suicide. The complex character of this doctor was played by Pankaj Kapur. Though the film showed the invention of a vaccine for leprosy instead of IVF, it depicted most of the issues faced by the real doctor: A committed man of science destroyed by a creaking bureaucratic machinery. How much did India lose because of the government's narrow-minded attitude? Well, Dr Robert Edwards, a British national, won the Nobel Prize in Medicine for inventing the IVF. If the Dr Mukhopadhyay had received the right support, he may have beaten Dr Edwards to it. The film delivers a hammer blow in driving this message home.

But one does not have to be a medical genius to save lives. Take Neerja Bhanot, for instance. She was not an ordinary person, in the strictest sense. A flight purser and a popular model visible across media (featuring in ads like Amul chocolates, Bajaj scooters and Parle biscuits), she was also the life and soul of her family. What made her extraordinary was the courage and presence of mind she demonstrated when, in 1986, the Pan Am aircraft in which she was on duty was hijacked by militants during a stopover in Karachi, Pakistan, en route from New Delhi to New York. In *Neerja* (2016), a film initially supported by the Bhanot family, Sonam Kapoor played the airhostess giving a strong performance that silenced her critics. The family, however, later sued the producer because the financial promises had not been met (they alleged that the producers had promised them 10 per cent of the film's profits, which they reneged on). The end result, regardless, was a faithful retelling of the thrilling tale of bravery and sacrifice that will live on people's memories for years to come.

In the complex and rich tapestry of India, there are a million stories waiting to be told. The madcap, multitalented genius Kishore Kumar is supposedly waiting to come alive in a biopic to be directed by Anurag Basu. It is rumoured that M.S. Dhoni will kick-start his film production company with a film on India's hockey wizard Dhyan Chand. A biopic on India's first (and only) man in space, Rakesh Sharma, is oscillating between Aamir Khan and Shah Rukh Khan playing him on screen. The wish list of biopics goes far beyond these, of course, but we know that most of them will see the light of day only if the film-makers who have envisioned them get the right stories written, find producers to back them and their living subjects (or the heirs of those departed) become less touchy about the way they are portrayed. While at it, I might as well ask for world peace!

## Ten historical biopics (some more legend than history)

***Sikandar*** **(1941):** Hindi cinema's doyen Prithviraj Kapoor played the title role while Sohrab Modi played his opposer Puru (or Porus). Released at the peak of the movement for freedom from British rule, the film roused strong nationalistic feelings among its audience.

***Baiju Bawra*** **(1952):** Bharat Bhushan played Baiju Bawra, the musician who was better than Tansen himself. The film's music topped all the charts.

***Taj Mahal*** **(1963):** Pradeep Kumar played the Mughal Emperor Shah Jahan, who sang brilliant songs on his way to building the grandest tomb of all time. (That sounds quite creepy, doesn't it!)

***Shatranj Ke Khilari*** **(1977):** Embedded in the tale of two chess players obsessed with their game while the world around them is in churn is the story of Nawab Wajid Ali Shah, the ruler of Awadh at the time of the kingdom's annexation by the British.

***Meera*** **(1979):** The story of Lord Krishna's greatest devotee was brought to the screen by Gulzar and Hema Malini, to the accompaniment of classic bhajans.

***Umrao Jaan*** **(1981):** Rekha took on the persona of the famous courtesan of 19th-century Lucknow, dressed in finery and mouthing sher-o-shayari.

***Razia Sultan*** **(1983):** The film about the only woman to ascend the throne of Delhi took longer to make than the sultana's reign. Kamal Amrohi directed the film and Hema Malini portrayed the legendary queen.

***Mangal Pandey: The Rising*** **(2005):** The man who triggered off the First War of Indian Independence in1857 became more heroic in the film version than any historical account ever suggested.

***Bajirao Mastani*** **(2015):** By all accounts, the Maratha Peshwa Bajirao married Mastani for political reasons, but in Sanjay Leela Bhansali's hands the story turned it into an all-heart, all-gloss saga that reflected very little of the real history.

***Padmaavat*** **(2018):** Bhansali's next foray about a queen of Chittorgarh in Mewar, who is most likely fictional provoked outrage among pockets of audiences at the portrayal of the queen in the film and obscured the fantastic fact that Deepika Padukone was paid more for the film than either of her male co-stars.

# 10

# YEH JO DESH HAI MERA

## A FILMI HISTORY OF INDEPENDENT INDIA

INDIA'S CHEQUERED HISTORY AFTER GAINING Independence from colonial rule has been marked by momentous events, quite a few of which have been recreated and reimagined in Hindi cinema. Audiences are divided on their favourites among these, depending on individual political ideologies and cinematic tastes, as the depictions of events have varied wildly. Some have been sober, measured and realistic, while others have been jingoistic, over-the-top and fantastical. That is, some are histories while others are simply, well, stories. Yet, if one were to take the broad view of the films in question, the key preoccupations of film-makers or the points of interest in India's history post 1947 come sharply into view.

## Partition

A struggle for freedom is almost without exception bloody and debilitating, but the birth of a new country brings peace, hope, reconstruction and renewal. Tragically, this did not hold true for India, as it saw the largest and bloodiest migration in human history when the British departed in 1947. The trauma of Partition probably held back film-makers from depicting its progress and aftermath on screen in the years that immediately followed the event. Though there were a few attempts – mostly low-key – to do so, and the occasional film mentioned it as something that was happening in the background, films largely steered clear of the Partition.

Then, in 1973, M.S. Sathyu's *Garm Hava* was released. It was one of the first films to be based entirely on the theme of the Partition and the grim realities that people faced at the time. Taking the assassination of Mahatma Gandhi (that is, a period 18 months after Partition) as its starting point, it examined the day-to-day problems of Indian Muslims who had chosen to stay back in India. They were faced with a depleting roster of friends and relatives, who were migrating to Pakistan fairly quickly, growing mistrust among fellow Indians (who were never sure of who would stay and who wouldn't) and governmental policies that were inadequate to meet the demands of the citizens of a newborn country. Balraj

Sahni played an upright elderly man anchored to old routines socially, in business and in his world view, while Farooq Sheikh played his younger son, idealistic and keen to adapt to the changing times and make a difference. The film was a balanced take on the entire spectrum of issues of the time. On the one hand, it questioned the archaic belief systems that certain groups of people clung to, while on the other hand, it strongly criticized the fledgling country's infrastructure for not being geared to help citizens in distress.

While *Garm Hava* ended on a positive note, it did not provide any relief from the horrors of Partition, if that was what audiences had hoped for. Many years later, in 2001, the unabashed happy ending, the punishing of the eternal 'enemy', Pakistan, and the grand unification of separated families as the two nations were born, were shown in unison in one loud, colourful saga called *Gadar: Ek Prem Katha*. The Sikh man-Muslim woman love story started in pre-1947 India and ended in post-Independence Pakistan, after Sunny Deol's character, Tara Singh, was shown laying waste to pretty much the entire country in an effort to bring his wife back home.

**Chinese Aggression**

The first historical 'mega' event after India's Independence would have to be the Sino-Indian War of 1962 – also

India's first major setback in terms of protecting its territory. The Chinese aggression to secure areas that the People's Republic of China considered its own was primarily a border dispute simmering since the McMahon Line was proposed by the British, but it was also triggered by India's decision to grant asylum to the Dalai Lama in 1959. Much has been said about India's diplomatic inability to anticipate Chinese action and the poor military choices made by the leadership at the time, but the bottom line was a defeat of Indian forces at the hands of the Chinese.

Almost immediately after the end of hostilities, Chetan Anand directed *Haqeeqat* (1964), which was based on the story of the fate of an Indian platoon caught between a rock and a hard place in the Ladakh area during this war. Hailed as the 'best Indian war film ever made' by many commentators, *Haqeeqat* showed how poor strategic decision-making (asking Indian soldiers to hold back till they didn't have a fighting chance left) manifested on the ground and led to battlefield heroics demonstrated by many of the soldiers. Ladakh's brutal terrain was shot marvellously (one is left wondering what the effect would have been if the film had been shot in colour) and the suffering of the soldiers, frostbitten and waiting interminably for orders to attack was poignantly depicted. *Haqeeqat* was a courageous film for attempting to tell a story from one of the darker chapters of India's history, as well as for its cinematography which adopted a hyper-realistic style in its depiction of the actual theatre of war. In a period when escapist romances ruled the box office, *Haqeeqat* injected some reality into the mix and ended up helping the post-war fundraising effort in a big way. (The film's signature song – 'Kar chale hum fida jaano o tan saathiyon, ab tumhare hawale watan saathiyon' – remains one of the most popular patriotic songs ever to be produced in Bollywood.)

The colour and grandeur that had been expected in *Haqeeqat* came more than 50 years later in Kabir Khan's *Tubelight* (2017), in which Salman Khan plays a slow learner, unable to understand why we fight wars. As his brother (Sohail Khan) joins the Indian war effort, Salman becomes the pacifist. The film is not so much about the war as it is about its fallout. While the film was lacking on several fronts, it was an interesting attempt to see the 1962 war through the prism of the hyper-nationalism prevalent in 2017.

**The Liberation of Bangladesh**

The 1971 war against Pakistan that brought about the the liberation of Bangladesh (then East Pakistan) was the first big-bang good news of post-Independence India. While India had fought a war against Pakistan in 1965 after an infiltration bid by the latter into Kashmir, no permanent territorial changes came about and the UN-mandated ceasefire did not indicate any clear victor. The year 1971 saw a calculated escalation of hostilities between the two countries, with then Prime Minister Indira Gandhi's declaration that it was more economical to go to war against Pakistan and assist erstwhile East Pakistan in its liberation than to take in a flood of refugees forced into India by Pakistan's atrocities in the east. The resultant victory led to Indira Gandhi being anointed as the demon-slaying goddess Durga by her peers, while the public signing of documents of surrender by the Pakistani generals left Pakistan with an embarrassing public image.

Based on these incidents, J.P. Dutta's *Border* can be called the Bollywood war film that pretty much defined the genre – layering a real war scenario with over-the-top action, melodrama, music and superior sound design. It depicted the Battle of Longewala fought during the 1971 War, in which a 'company' of 120 soldiers held back a Pakistani infantry brigade of more than 2000 soldiers and tanks. The real-life battle was heroic enough, and with Sunny Deol, Suniel Shetty, Akshaye Khanna, Puneet Issar, Kulbhushan Kharbanda and other such worthies (not to forget Jackie Shroff in a guest appearance) added to the mix, it was quite the uplifting experience. The film ended with a message about pacifism and the futility of war, but derived its massive popularity from the adrenaline-laden battle scenes and jingoistic dialogues.

On the other hand, Amrit Sagar's *1971* (2007) was an unusual take on the 1971 War, because it was set six years after the war ended. It was the story of six prisoners of war trying to escape from Pakistan, where they were being held hostage without any record or reason. While the story was largely fictional, it raised the issue of 54 missing Indian soldiers long suspected to have been held as prisoners of war in Pakistan – a less reported but extremely poignant part of India's history.

**The Emergency**

All the goodwill that Indira Gandhi generated after the victory of 1971 was lost in a maze of rampant corruption, poor human development indices and the extreme poverty that prevailed in the country during her reign as prime minister. This led to massive discontentment among large sections of the population with open protests against her policies being launched by veteran freedom fighter Jayaprakash Narayan, among others. To make matters worse, she was found guilty of electoral malpractices by the Allahabad High Court. Her fear of potential imprisonment and losing her position of power led to her declaring a state of Emergency in

June 1975 – plunging the country into probably the darkest chapter in its democracy.

When considering the films that featured the Emergency, one has to talk about Amrit Nahata's *Kissa Kursi Ka*, a spoof on Sanjay Gandhi, Indira Gandhi's elder son, and his coterie. Originally submitted for certification in April 1975, the film's prints mysteriously disappeared after the Emergency was declared. It was later discovered that the prints had been taken to the Maruti factory (which was being operated by Sanjay Gandhi) and burned. The Shah Commission, which was set up to investigate the excesses of the Emergency, found Sanjay Gandhi and his accomplices guilty of criminal conspiracy and causing disappearance of evidence, among other heavy charges, but this could not bring the original film back from the ashes. The film-maker remade the film and released it in 1977, though the content of the film didn't match up to the hype. In a plot somewhat marred by the high symbolism it attempted, Shabana Azmi played a deaf and mute character (representing democracy) being taken advantage of by politicians at every juncture. With the target of the black humour no longer in power, the impact of the satire was diluted and the film didn't do too well – either commercially or critically.

The Emergency became a very sensitive topic for the Congress, which effectively stopped it from being the subject of a viable film when the party returned to power in 1979. It was years before the Emergency cropped up again, though only in a tangential reference, in Sudhir Mishra's *Hazaaron Khwaishein Aisi* (2003), a film about a motley group of students who follow different ideological persuasions after their graduation. The wave of Naxal protests against capitalist ideologies that overwhelmed the country in 1969 had slowly given way to the corruption of the early years of the next decade that witnessed the Emergency midway through it. The wheeler-dealers, that is, the elite indulging in crony capitalism, and the abject helplessness of the poor were portrayed through a layer of satire and served up coated in a veneer of anonymity to avoid political wrath. For one thing, the characters in the film who somewhat resembled real-life people did not appear at the points in history they belonged to and were not shown to be in complicity with the Emergency in any way. For instance, a Sanjay Gandhi lookalike appears in 1973 and is more interested in dealmakers rather than – say – sterilizers![6]

Madhur Bhandarkar's *Indu Sarkar* (2017), however, made no such pretence. Released at a time when the Congress party was not in power, the film cast Neil Nitin Mukesh as Sanjay Gandhi and Supriya Vinod as Indira

[6] Another Sanjay Gandhi lookalike popped up in *Baadshaho* (2017), as a character who, after being insulted by a princess in Rajasthan, triggers the heist that is the central point of the film.

Gandhi presiding over a chaotic mess of corruption and cruelty even as a bunch of idealistic crusaders take up arms against them. Offsetting the subtlety of *Hazaaron Khwaishein Aisi*, *Indu Sarkar* was like a sledgehammer – choosing to portray on a broad canvas pretty much all the excesses of the times. The stammering crusader (the eponymous Indu Sarkar, played by Kirti Kulhari) turns out to be a legendary – albeit fictional – character taking up arms in a completely unrealistic way in a film that, ironically, starts off with the claim of being realistic.

### The Anti-Sikh Riots and Insurgency in the Punjab

Indira Gandhi returned to power in 1979 and was all set to retain the majority in 1984 when she ordered Operation Blue Star (in June 1984) to flush out Sikh terrorists from the Golden Temple. The resultant damage to the shrine led to massive outrage among and the alienation of the Sikh community. The immediate fallout of the incident was the assassination of Indira Gandhi by her Sikh bodyguards which, in turn, led to widespread 'revenge' killings of Sikhs across the country. Operation Blue Star and the anti-Sikh riots that followed the assassination of Indira Gandhi pretty much kicked off the violent cycle of terrorism and state action that lasted for several years in the Punjab.

Shonali Bose's *Amu* (2005) was a thoughtful exploration of the Sikh riots from the perspective of a non-resident Indian (NRI) woman who starts investigating it several years later. Konkona Sen Sharma plays the young woman who uncovers a personal connection to the 1984 massacre. The film presented an interesting juxtaposition of her deep connection with the violence and the world's detached view of an event that was never discussed in India as much it should have been. Sadly, in a pattern that's becoming all too predictable before a film's release, the film ran into issues with censor certification. The censor board had references to the riots removed in several places and certified it as an 'adult' film, making it that much more difficult for many viewers to access it.

Gulzar's *Maachis* (1996), set in the Punjab of the late 1980s, is a brutal story of the mindless cycle of terrorist and police action, and the violations of humanity on both sides. The film had a stellar cast of Tabu, Om Puri and Kulbhushan Kharbanda, along with newcomers Jimmy Shergill and Chandrachur Singh playing a group of youngsters in terrorism-hit Punjab. The film showed how even the most ordinary actions may quickly lead to violent repercussions, which made the superbly drawn out script all the more moving and disturbing. Gulzar has often taken up highly political subjects, mixing criticism and satire in his treatment of them. *Maachis* was a cynical outing, even by his standards, in which he firmly communicated his world view that there are no heroes or villains in the fight against terrorism, nor are there any winners.

**Terrorism in Kashmir**

By the late 1980s, while terrorism in Punjab had started to die out, Kashmir was ready to explode. Kashmir has always been something of a time bomb, ever since the state joined the Indian Union in 1947 and received a special status from the Indian government. Many promises made by the Indian government to its people never became a reality, leading to simmering discontent among the population. This reached a flashpoint when the 1987 elections in the state were declared as having been rigged in favour of the coalition between the Farooq Abdullah-led National Conference party and the Congress party. The ISI, Pakistan's intelligence agency, fuelled the discontent on the ground with arms, ammunition and the Islamic radicalization of Kashmir's people, especially its youth, leading to widespread insurgency within the state that had tragic and frightening repercussions across the country. Police and army brutality were reported on real and alleged terrorists, who – in turn – were responsible for engineering the large-scale exodus of the Kashmiri Pandit population from the state.

Vidhu Vinod Chopra's *Mission Kashmir* (2000) was a part-nostalgic, part-fantastic view of the Kashmir problem. As someone who had grown up in the state, Chopra had a slightly rose-tinted view of the solution, resulting in a true-blue masala film involving a police officer (Sanjay Dutt) and his foster son (Hrithik Roshan), who found themselves fighting on opposite sides before good sense prevailed. The film, ultimately, was all about the power of *Kashmiriyat* and how Hindu–Muslim unity would eventually defeat the divisive forces.

Vishal Bhardwaj's *Haider* (2014) was probably the antithesis of *Mission Kashmir* in the way it depicted the Kashmir issue. Placing the plot of Shakespeare's *Hamlet* in present-day Kashmir, it was a bleak look at the way the Indian army had lost the trust of the common people of the state with their deal-making, brutality and lack of empathy. Bhardwaj collaborated with Kashmiri journalist Basharat Peer to create the screenplay based on Peer's personal experiences of growing up in a state torn by terrorism. Shahid Kapoor delivered the performance of a lifetime as he swung between cooperating with the terrorists and the security forces (and their allies within his family) and not knowing whom to trust – reflecting the dilemma among Kashmiris themselves.

### The Demolition of the Babri Masjid and Its Aftermath

The dispute involving the property designated as 'Ram

Janmabhoomi' on which the Babri Masjid stands was rekindled in 1986 when the mosque's gates were unlocked to give Hindus access to the land, making the demands for a temple at the location more strident. This demand turned into a nationwide campaign when L.K. Advani, a senior leader of the Bharatiya Janata Party (BJP), travelled across the entire country on a 'rath yatra' demanding that the disputed land be handed over to Hindus for the worship of Lord Ram. The accretion of the primarily politicized Hindu demands for a temple led to an attack on the mosque on 6 December 1992, when it was broken down by *kar sevaks* and the followers of the Rashtriya Swayamsevak Sangh (RSS). The resultant backlash led to widespread incidents of Hindu-Muslim riots, the worst of which probably broke out in Mumbai where the Shiv Sena, a regional nationalist party, held sway. The aftermath of that one afternoon in Ayodhya lasted several months (and years), costing countless lives, large-scale destruction of property and an almost irrevocable loss of trust between the two communities.

Mani Ratnam's *Bombay* (1995) was his grand paean to romantic love in times of religious isolation as Arvind Swamy and Manisha Koirala played a Hindu-Muslim couple trying to bring up their twin sons in a riot-ridden Bombay in 1992. Starting the story in a nondescript Indian village opposed to an inter-religious marriage, the film took the couple to Bombay. The city afforded them the anonymity they craved till riots broke out, endangering their two children, who were neither Hindu nor Muslim in the day's terminology. *Bombay* went through its share of controversy over the name itself (because the city had become Mumbai while the film was set in Bombay) and its portrayal of the events. The Shiv Sena objected to the depiction of their leader, Bal Thackeray, and of his role in the riots. Remarkably, Thackeray did not object to the film showing a character similar to him instigating the riots – rather, he was upset about the character feeling remorse at the end. He openly claimed that he didn't regret anything that had happened under his watch.

In the same year released Saeed Akhtar Mirza's *Naseem* (1995), a small film quite the antithesis in scale to *Bombay*, that had a completely different perspective on the same events. It also had a very unusual lead pair – a storytelling grandfather and his school-going granddaughter, played by the legendary poet Kaifi Azmi (in his only acting role) and debutant Mayuri Kango respectively. Returning to the grandfather's life story in flashback, the film counterpointed friendlier times in India's history with the atmosphere in Bombay just before December 1992. It was a despairing look at the communal turn the city had taken. The film was critically acclaimed and awarded the National Award for Best Direction and Screenplay, but did not reach a wide audience.

### The Kargil War

The Kargil War (May 1999–July 1999) was the first large-scale military action to have broken out after 1971 and for the majority of the Indian population of the time it was the first war they ever experienced. It was also the first televised war and journalists seemed to be as much a part of the action as the soldiers. The bravery of the soldiers, the magnitude of their sacrifices, their use of advertising slogans to initiate military action were reported in real time and the nation had a ringside view of the action. It was also the first time that junior officers were given key responsibilities and they stepped up to the task by literally leading from the front. The Kargil War saw a very high proportion of officers being martyred alongside jawans.

After the success of *Border*, J.P. Dutta made *LOC: Kargil* (2003), which promptly laid claim to several records – the longest running time (4 hours 15 minutes), the largest star cast (featuring pretty much every star of the time), the longest song ('Main kahin bhi rahoon…'), the highest shooting location, and so on. While the sincerity of the effort was never in doubt, *LOC: Kargil* remains an unwieldy, overly long, largely impersonal sequence of events that didn't quite capture the drama of the war, the tragedy of loss or the euphoria of victory.

In fact, the film that captured all these quite well didn't even mention Kargil as a location and passed itself off as a fictional film. Depending on how you look at it, Farhan Akhtar's *Lakshya* (2004) was either told from the perspective of an aimless youth who transforms into a responsible soldier, or from the perspective of an idealistic student who battles gender prejudice to become a star reporter. The story had its real-life parallels but used fiction beautifully to depict the millennial generation's experience of the first major challenge in their time to India's territorial integrity. The war featured in only the last one-third of the film and it was as much a coming-of-age film as it was a war film. In its last moments, the commendation from a parent of a son who had done him proud held as much importance as the unfurling of the tricolour on a snow-clad peak, declaring victory.

### The Riots in Gujarat

While victory in the Kargil War proved to be the high point for the country's first non-Congress government, enabling it to last a full term in office, the 2002 riots that tore Gujarat apart certainly marked the lowest. It catapulted Gujarat's then chief minister, Narendra Modi, into the limelight and the debate about his role in the riots continues even today. What cannot be debated, though, is that there was a state-wide attack on Muslims in Gujarat – as 'revenge' for an attack on a train carrying a group of *kar sevaks* – and thousands of people were killed, raped and dispossessed of everything they owned. The riots also led to considerable polarization among the media, with supporters and opponents taking extreme views of the state's role in the riots.

Nandita Das's *Firaaq* (2008) was an anthology of four stories through which she looked at how different people from different strata of society behaved during the riots. The film examined closely the problems of isolation, mistrust and corruption that arise as a by-product of communal violence. As is the norm with such films in India, no political leader or party was named as the perpetrator of the attacks, instead, the film focused on the victimization of Muslims during the riots. The film was a hard, uncompromising look at the violence that took place, with no easy answers offered or attempts made to sugarcoat the message.

Abhishek Kapoor's *Kai Po Che* (2013), on the other hand, took the popular route and placed three very likeable characters in the middle of the riot. It, too, didn't name parties or leaders but gave enough historical pointers (in the form of cricket matches) to fix the exact time, location and circumstances around which the story was constructed. The film portrayed the riots and their aftermath with a great degree of hope, providing a light at the end of the tunnel by conveying the message that, in the end, humanity triumphs over all.

### The 2011 ICC World Cup Victory

The occasions in history that we consider momentous tend to be wars, assassinations, mass migrations, natural calamities – events that inspire fear or sadness. India's history is no exception. Yet, there are moments of triumph and success at individual levels that bring us ecstasy, joy and fulfilment, and many of these are connected to sports.

In 2011, when a former ticket collector from Ranchi slammed a delivery from a Sri Lankan fast bowler into the stands of Mumbai's Wankhede Stadium for a six, it was probably modern India's happiest moment. India's previous cricket World Cup win had come 28 years earlier, even before India's cricket team had a significant following. In terms of being transformative, the Indian cricket team's victory in 1983 was probably a more significant one because it kicked off a journey that culminated in India's superpower status in cricket – but it is yet to get a proper ode in cinema. Nagesh Kukunoor's *Iqbal* (2005) paid a tribute to the 1983 win in a scene showing the hero's mother going into labour just as India wins the final match and being blessed with a son with the potential to engineer another such win.

Recently, director Kabir Khan has announced a film on the 1983 victory with Ranveer Singh playing Kapil Dev – only time will tell if it will hit the mark.

The 2011 win was more like the fulfilment of a nation's collective dream, the culmination of a nearly three-decade-long wait for victory. Moreover, this journey had two heroes. The first was, of course, the team's captain M.S. Dhoni. Dhoni's journey from the government quarters of Ranchi to the Indian cricket team alone is the stuff dreams are made of. But Dhoni is nothing if not a great finisher. His biopic, *M.S. Dhoni: The Untold Story* (2016), started with a scene showing the day of the World Cup final and flashbacked into his origins, essentially telling the story of millions of India's small-town boys and girls who break away from their humble beginnings to reach unprecedented heights. More than the cricketing milestones, it was the chronicle of an aspirational and ambitious young man's battle against the poor infrastructure, apathetic support system and lack of exposure that affect the lives and futures of thousands of talented youth in India today.

The other man's journey to the World Cup had an air of inevitability about it. The 'world's greatest batsman' couldn't retire without cricket's greatest prize, after all. All of Sachin Tendulkar's runs and records were deemed inconsequential when the country looked longingly at the imaginary place in the hypothetical trophy cabinet that existed in every Indian's mind. *Sachin: A Billion Dreams* (2017) was not a feature film but a satisfying tribute to the genius cricketer's journey from being a child prodigy playing under the supervision of his brother at Shivaji Park to a living legend hoisted on his team's shoulders in a stadium about 12 kilometres away from his neighbourhood, as the crow flies. But it took him – and the rest of India – millions of kilometres of touring, hundreds of kilometres of running, and hours of practice and prayer to get there. Many commentators have said that Sachin is the first cricketer of post-liberalization India. He didn't believe in the fixed deposit scheme of gathering runs slowly. Instead, he dabbled in mutual funds that yielded explosive run fests. The documentary traced his – and India's – journey to the final coveted destination, after climbing every other mountain across the world where they'd played cricket. In a way, this film on Sachin didn't just trace his life but that of every post-liberalization kid who, thanks to a mix of hard work and opportunities, scaled – in their own modest ways – peaks similar to those ascended by the curly-haired boy from Shivaji Park. In a way, the film was their biopic as well.

Quite like a glass that is half full and half empty at the same time, there are two ways of looking at any event. One can see it as the beginning of an end – the end of secularism, the victory of terrorism, the isolation of a people. Or it could be the beginning of something beautiful – the emergence of faith, the discovery of courage, the genesis of new relationships. Hindi cinema – though not always partial to reality – has always looked at things from both perspectives. For every life sacrificed at the front, there are several heroes going home victorious. For every victim of terror, there are many bringing justice to the victims. For every child killed in a riot, there are several who grow up to be model citizens. Much like life, that is.

And, if there aren't, then there is always the sequel. *Kyunki,* picture *abhi baaki hai, mere dost.*

# SOURCES AND BIBLIOGRAPHY


Anand, Dev, *Romancing with Life*, New Delhi: Penguin Books India, 2011.

Bhatia, Sidharth, *Amar Akbar Anthony: Masala, Madness and Manmohan Desai,* New Delhi: HarperCollins Publishers India, 2013.

Bhattacharjee, Anirudha and Balaji Vittal, *R.D. Burman: The Man, The Music*, New Delhi: HarperCollins Publishers India, 2011.

Bose, Mihir, *Bollywood: A History*, Ireland: Tempus Publishing Ltd, 2006.

Chopra, Anupama, *Sholay: The Making of a Classic*, New Delhi: Penguin Books India, 2000.

Christo, Bob, *Flashback: My Life and Times in Bollywood and Beyond,* New Delhi: Penguin Books India, 2011.

Gulzar, *Pantabhatey* [Bengali], Kolkata: Ananda Publishers, 2017.

Kapoor, Rishi and Meena Iyer, *Khullam Khulla: Rishi Kapoor Uncensored*, New Delhi: HarperCollins Publishers India, 2017.

Kothari, Jigna and Supriya Madangarli, *Gangs of Wasseypur: The Making of a Modern Classic,* New Delhi: HarperCollins Publishers India, 2013.

Kumar, Dilip, *The Substance and the Shadow: An Autobiography*, New Delhi: Hay House India, 2014.

Manto, Saadat Hasan translated by Khalid Hasan, *Stars from Another Sky: The Bombay Film World of the 1940s*, New Delhi: Penguin Books India, 2010.

Manwani, Akshay, *Sahir Ludhianvi: The People's Poet*, New Delhi: HarperCollins Publishers India, 2013.

Mehra, Rakeysh Omprakash, Kamlesh Pandey and Rensil D'Silva, *Rang De Basanti: The Shooting Script,* Om Books International, 2014.

Nanda, Ritu, *Raj Kapoor Speaks*, New Delhi: Penguin Books India, 2002.

Pinto, Jerry, *Helen: The Life and Times of a Bollywood H-Bomb,* New Delhi: Penguin Books India, 2006.

Saran, Sathya, *Ten Years with Guru Dutt: Abrar Alvi's Journey*, New Delhi: Penguin Books India, 2011.

Singh, Jai Arjun, *Jaane Bhi Do Yaaro: Seriously Funny Since 1983*, New Delhi: HarperCollins Publishers India, 2010.

Stadtman, Todd, *Funky Bollywood: The Wild World of 1970s Indian Action Cinema,* United Kingdom: FAB Press, 2015.

Usman, Yasser, *Rekha: The Untold Story*, New Delhi: Juggernaut Books, 2016.

Zaidi, S. Hussain, *Dongri to Dubai: Six Decades of the Mumbai Mafia*, New Delhi: Lotus, 2012.

Zankar, Anil, *Mughal-e-Azam: Legend as Epic*, New Delhi: Harper Collins Publishers India, 2013.

# ACKNOWLEDGEMENTS

Books like this (read, all the books I write) stand on the shoulders of many helpful giants:

Abhishek Paul, who shared his perspectives of Indian history and helped me contextualize some of the references to pop culture.

Aneela Z. Babar, who was her usual ebullient self while recounting stories of watching Bollywood films in Pakistan. And elsewhere.

Anirban Banerjee, whose thoughts on Hindi film music (which run perpendicular to mine) were invaluable in shaping some of the chapters.

Parth Pandya and Suhel Banerjee, who brought their twin identities – Hindi cinema fans and book lovers – to critique some of the chapter drafts.

Poulomi Chatterjee, who was the perfect editor. She brought the idea to me, left me free to write it the way

I wanted to and smoothly tied up the loose ends to create the final book.

Thomas Abraham, who was the perfect publisher. When not discussing film quizzes, he threw a slew of book ideas my way. Hopefully, some of them will get converted into real books.

Trishna, Dyujoy and Drishti Chaudhuri, who were their usual stoic selves as I went about re-re-re-watching 1970s films on YouTube and changing radio channels to Hindi retro.

While writing any book or even thinking about one, a writer's greatest assets are a fount of ideas and a sounding board. Over the last couple of years, I have found the perfect group of people who have encouraged my good ideas, mocked the bad ones and thrown many more at me that I have later claimed as my own. Their contribution to this book has been much more than they will ever realize.

It is my honour and privilege to dedicate this book to The WhatsApp Group that Doesn't Forward Jokes.